PATH TO
ZERO

PATH TO
ZERO

12 CLIMATE CONVERSATIONS
THAT CHANGED THE WORLD

TUCKER PERKINS

Worth

Published by Worth Books, Nashville, Tennessee.

Distributed by Simon & Schuster.

Library of Congress Control Number: 2024910319

Print ISBN: 978-1-63763-308-3
E-book ISBN: 978-1-63763-309-0

Cover Design by George Stevens, G Sharp Design LLC
Interior Design by Mary Susan Oleson, Blu Design Concepts

Printed in the United States of America

For everyone's great-great-grandchildren

Contents

FOREWORD
by MEREDITH ANGWIN 9

INTRODUCTION:
WHEN NARRATIVES REPLACE CONVERSATIONS.....................13

CHAPTER 1: SILVER BUCKSHOT 19
Path to Zero Conversation #1: Katharine Hayhoe 29

CHAPTER 2: LIQUID ENERGY FOR EVERYONE 37
Path to Zero Conversation #2: Kevin Lucke 43
Path to Zero Conversation #3: Richard Palmer......................49

CHAPTER 3: FROM ESG TO 3-D 57
Path to Zero Conversation #4: Jeffrey Schlegelmilch..............69
Path to Zero Conversation #5: Michael Burr 77

CHAPTER 4: DIESEL'S LAST DECADE.....................................87
Path to Zero Conversation #6:
Felix Leach and Kelly Senecal 93

CHAPTER 5: ENERGY, ECONOMY, ENVIRONMENT 111
Path to Zero Conversation #7: Scott Tinker 113

CHAPTER 6: THE ENERGY OF THE FUTURE 127
Path to Zero Conversation #8, #9, #10, #11, #12:
Robert Bryce, Meredith Angwin, Sir Steven Cowley,
Dr. Rusty Towell, Dr. Steven Koonin 131

CHAPTER 7: MAGIC WANDS AND A CRYSTAL BALL.................147

CONCLUSION:
WHEN CONVERSATIONS REPLACE NARRATIVES......................169

ACKNOWLEDGMENTS 177
PATH TO ZERO **EPISODES BY SEASON** 179
NOTES 201
INDEX..229

Foreword
by Meredith Angwin

Tucker Perkins has a superpower: he sees the future by listening in the present. On his *Path to Zero* podcast, Perkins invites scores of experts, each with a different view about climate change and energy. In this book, he uses these statements to predict the energy sources for 2050.

I was pleased to be on his podcast. I agree with Tucker's assertion that "there's no clean energy silver bullet. There's only silver buckshot." We will use a variety of sources and strategies to build the energy future. Another way to describe the necessary mix of energy sources is that "there's no single right answer; there are only trade-offs."

For example, some people don't believe baseload exists. But it does. Baseload is the electricity required by the grid 24/7. On most power grids, this always-required baseload is 60 percent or more of the electricity used each day. The baseload electricity needs to be steady, reliable, and nonpolluting.

However, it does not need to be fast-acting. Requiring fast response for baseload power sources is the same as requiring great acceleration from semitrucks. Neither the baseload units nor semitrucks are designed for that kind of service. Similarly, high-performance sports cars are not designed for hauling heavy cargo cross-country. Different designs created for different purposes.

The powerful message of this book is that many types of primary energy can contribute to a healthy future. Clean petroleum products like propane can help isolated and poor areas avoid deforestation in search of biomass and avoid lung disease in people from indoor air pollution. Later, these areas can be connected to the electric grid. Nuclear energy has low pollution and high reliability. It can displace coal for baseload power in the next decade.

The energy tradeoffs will differ according to the situation. Prosperous countries can deploy small modular nuclear power to support the baseload. Less prosperous countries with few people connected to the grid can make choices proportional to their needs.

In this book, you will hear from people who appreciate the role that hydrocarbons have played in lifting much of the world out of extreme poverty and from others who eagerly look forward to the fusion future. Yet the underlying theme continues: the world needs continuous improvement, not sudden epiphanies.

Conversations are important. In many venues, I might try to say that I think we should cut back on carbon, but carbon isn't the only issue for the future. I might try to emphasize "trade-offs, not miracles." Some people would immediately call me a climate denier. Others would listen to the same statement and call me a climate alarmist. However, name-calling does not help. We need a conversation.

I am grateful that Tucker listens to me, as he listens to everyone. He encourages us to use our most valuable resources—communication and problem-solving. Communication and problem-solving are the deep themes of this book.

When Narratives Replace Conversations

Perfect is the enemy of good.

— VOLTAIRE

In early 2023, members of the Energy and Policy Institute, an electrify-everything advocacy group, attended a meeting of the Propane Education and Research Council (PERC). After listening to a debate among council members concerning climate change, electrification, and energy alternatives, the group contacted a *New York Times* reporter named Hiroko Tabuchi. They told Tabuchi that the Council had plans to "spend $13 million on [an] anti-electrification campaign."

Tabuchi's article alleged that PERC was anti-electrification, was spending money on anti-electrification messaging in violation of its congressional charter, and was a climate change–denying organization.[1]

None of this was true, but that didn't stop a half dozen other news outlets from syndicating the article and repeating the false narrative without even bothering to ask. I even had one would-be guest, a journalist, cancel their appearance on my podcast, citing Tabuchi's story as the reason.

Over the past several years, I have hosted a wide range of industry thought leaders and experts on the topic of clean energy and the journey toward a low-carbon future. I have had fundamental disagreements with some of them, but at least we sat and talked to each other. This cancellation was a first for me.

I had an Anthony Bourdain quote swimming in my head when all this happened: "*Listen* to someone you think may have nothing in common with you. . . . Be open to a world where you may not understand or agree with the person next to you but have a drink with them anyway."[2]

In writing this book, I invite readers to be open to a world where you may not agree with me. I come from a hydrocarbon background, having spent a career in the propane industry as a distributor, marketer, and now as the leader of the industry's congressionally chartered research and education arm. I imagine—in fact I hope—readers of this book come from all different backgrounds and perspectives on energy and climate change.

Today, narratives like "electrify everything" have a grip on people's minds. It is human nature to be easily seduced by seemingly simple solutions to complex problems, so I would like to start off by asking you to agree to a few key principles:

- The transition to a net zero future is the most complex challenge ever faced by humans. Seeing patterns is essential. Blind spots and biases keep us from spotting what may be obvious.

- A perfectly clean energy source with zero conversion consequences does not exist. We are in, therefore, a conversation involving imperfect trade-offs, but the good news is that as we make trade-offs, we can, in fact, make better and better choices.

- The conversations I have had on *Path to Zero*—ninety-nine and counting—have convinced me that graciously exchanging ideas and debating points of view about the choices ahead is essential.

While I try to persuade you regarding the principles above, let's appreciate the perspectives of climate activists like former US vice president Al Gore and Greta Thunberg, philanthropists like Bill Gates, journalists like Elizabeth Kolbert, General Secretary of the United Nations António Guterres, the Intergovernmental Panel on Climate Change (IPCC), and even 350.org founder, Bill McKibben. While we may not agree on everything, we share a sense of urgency for reducing carbon and greenhouse gas emissions as quickly as possible.

One more perspective to consider is that of early-twentieth-century journalist and writer H. L. Mencken, who said, "For every complex problem there is an answer that is clear, simple, and wrong."[3]

A few years ago, a mentor and friend of mine, Bob Myers, a longtime leader in the propane industry, told a small group of us, "Today, the all-electrification herd is in a stampede. If we try to stop it, we'll get trampled to death." To a person, none of us on the call wanted to be trampled. Thankfully, Bob gave us a gentle but powerful nudge by recognizing that when scientific facts are being overridden by moral certitude, we may be able to "turn the herd" if we work hard to find a better way forward.

The wide path toward a net zero emissions future is that turn.

The wide path includes massive shifts toward electrification (though we ought to be fully aware that electricity is not an energy source; it is a transmission method).

The wide path includes the expansion of intermittent renewables such as solar and wind. The wide path includes a sincere effort to find a way to manufacture hydrogen that is both green and affordable. On the wide path, innovators in small modular nuclear reactors are welcome, as are the pioneers inching closer to the promise of nuclear fusion. Hydro- and geo-power innovators are wide-path fellows, as are technologists working every day to imagine better engines and batteries that don't require the earth-ravaging mining of rare earth elements like nickel, cobalt, and lithium.

Wide-path advocates are not anti-electrification. We are pro-decarbonization. We believe climate change is real and that many solutions to it are better than one.

If we can strive for objectivity over bias, we can collaborate to achieve real change that will lead to a sustainable future for all.

To power that future, we need energy with the lowest possible carbon intensity; we need energy production proximate to its usage for maximum efficiency; we need energy devoid of health consequences; and we need energy with equity—reliable, affordable, and accessible to everyone. Sustainable solutions cannot just be for people who can afford to move elsewhere. The wide path must be open to everyone.

Consider electric vehicles like Tesla. Who benefits from a Tesla passenger vehicle that can cost $75,000? Are electric vehicles important in the energy transition? Yes. But does a Tesla meet all of the requirements listed above for a sustainable energy future? No. It is neither an affordable nor an accessible solution for the masses. In fact, the people who probably benefit the least from these vehicles (because they cannot access them financially) are the same people who live nearest the coal-burning power plants generating the electricity to send to the charging stations—a fact often skipped over by Tesla's carbon-free marketing.

The wide path is filled with optimism. We can reverse and adapt to the effects of climate change if we muster the courage to work together. In the pages to come, I'll uncover an array of practical, and often obvious, steps the world can take toward a cleaner future. In that sense, this is likely one of the most practical books on climate change you will read.

Change is possible, not just for me and not just for you, but for our children and our grandchildren, and for their children and grandchildren after them. The time is now. If *we* don't do it, I don't think it will get done. We are envisioning an outcome we may never see, but it's something we can care deeply about in our time. If you're reading this book, I imagine you are among those who share this conviction. I hope you will walk away with an optimism you can share with others.

Is it possible to achieve a net zero emissions future? Absolutely. In fact, I'm going to show you how we will do it by the year 2050.

In each chapter that follows, we will fast-forward nearly three decades to an imagined history of how we achieved net zero in such a short period of time. I propose that by 2050 our hard work has paid off, we've achieved zero emissions, and some of the poorest nations in the world are now thriving because of how we did it.

How can we make this speculative history a reality? You're about to find out. As the saying goes, every journey begins with a first step. So it is as we venture down the wide path.

CHAPTER 1

Silver Buckshot

Optimism is a strategy for making a better future.
Because unless you believe that the future can
be better, you are unlikely to step up and
take responsibility for making it so.
— NOAM CHOMSKY

Kaizen is a Japanese word coined in 1986 by Masaaki Imai in his book *Kaizen: The Key to Japan's Competitive Success.* In the United States, the word has been adopted to connote an attitude of continuous improvement. The Kaizen Way is expressed as "improving the world with everyone, everywhere, every day."

Think about the profound implications of that perspective. If we can align on purpose, values, and long-term goals, nothing is impossible. If we can understand data and create transparent information that can easily be shared with others,

19

we will share the positive outcomes. We can leverage the insights and ideas of visionaries. Rather than marginalize skeptics, we can harness their power to help us address problems from different points of view. We can eliminate waste, improve processes, and renew vast and complex systems with quality and growth. Kaizen means that we can and should do a thousand things better to create collective advantage.

To add to this thought, Taiichi Ohno, known as the Father of the Toyota Production System, said: "Standards should not be forced down from above but rather set by the production workers themselves." In this quote, Ohno reminds us that doing a thousand things better also involves a thousand people, metaphorically speaking. Companies like Toyota have made kaizen a centerpiece of their culture. Toyota's sustained success—it has now been the number one or number two carmaker in the world for well over a decade—is in no small part a result of the persistent application of kaizen philosophy.[1]

Today, Toyota is once again taking a leadership position at the center of the climate change conversation. It's not because the company has followed the pack of global auto manufacturers over the electrification cliff. Instead, Toyota has held firm in its belief that hybrid vehicles equipped with high-efficiency internal combustion engines (ICE) and electric motors that are charged by the engine while driving are the key to a successful energy transition in the transportation sector.

Why is Toyota so committed to the hybrid approach?

Three reasons explain their hesitation toward the mass-market adoption of electrified vehicles: charging infrastructure, charging times, and concerns about EV load on the electric grid.

Charging Infrastructure

Charging infrastructure is a problem.[2] Available charging stations number about 130,000 across the United States. Comparatively, the federal government estimates there are about 168,000 fueling stations in the country, each with an average of eight pumps, equaling 1,344,000 places to refuel.[3] The scarcity of electric vehicle charging stations will diminish over time, but not quickly. Level 2 chargers, usually found at public charging stations pulling power from the grid, cost between $1,200 and $6,000 by most accounts.[4] Quick math tells us that we need as much as $7,284,000,000 of investment to make the number of EV charging stations as accessible as gas pumps.

According to the White House, the 2022 Inflation Reduction Act allocated $7.5 billion in tax credits to incentivize the installation of more EV charging stations, which means private entities must first invest the funds and then apply for tax reduction based on the invested capital.[5] It's going to take several years of work to get the plumbing straightened out for the money to actually flow. Toyota's assumption is that hybrid vehicles will be more attractive while infrastructure gets installed.

Charging Times

Toyota believes in the hybrid vehicle approach because of charging times. Try this thirty-second test: Search online for an answer to the question "How long does it take to charge an electric car?" You are likely to return with a variety of responses that all hang on the phrase "it depends." One report sums up the dilemma by saying, "The size of an EV's battery, its efficiency, its onboard charger, and the power source itself are among the many variables at play."[6] The weather, the temperature of the battery pack, and even the quality of the charging cable are also variables that prevent a clear answer to the question.

Easy-to-understand tables related to charging times (when they can be found) show that using a standard-issue 240V commercial Level 2 charger, an EV takes between two and five hours to fully charge, but the variables above make this a best-guess situation.[7] How about a real-world test?

In June 2022, reporter Rachel Wolfe did just that. She wrote a detailed article about her 2,000-mile road trip from New Orleans to Chicago.[8] Finding chargers was difficult in spite of an app promising to guide her to available fast units, including those at car dealerships. That frustration was compounded by charging time variability. At her stopover in Meridian, Mississippi, her battery took three hours to fully recharge. A better equipped dealership in Birmingham, Alabama, completed the recharge process in about an hour. Rachel navigated through mountain roads bereft of charging stations—a segment of the trip she referred to as "EV hazing." She completed the next segment of her trip with recharge times as low as twenty-five minutes, then revisited the three-hour charge time after watching her battery life rapidly decline while driving through a thunderstorm.

The first line of Wolfe's nail-biting story reads: "I thought it would be fun." The subhead of the piece underscores the takeaway: "She wouldn't soon do it again."

Think for a moment about hitting the road and having to factor in multi-hour charging times along any substantive journey. Add in some hot weather, ornery family members, and perhaps a passenger's pre-existing medical condition, and you've got yourself a recipe for a meltdown.

Increased Load on the Grid

The electric grid isn't ready for wide-scale electric vehicle adoption. It is not difficult to find warnings from objective sources about the challenges that EV adoption poses for the grid in the form of expensive, last-minute upgrades to compensate for widespread additional charger load.

David Ferris wrote in a June 2023 article, "When millions of cars migrate from liquid fuel to electric current, the changes can be profound. . . . Consequences appear that no one ever anticipated, in places no one thought to look."[9]

Ferris goes on to quote Ryan Quint, an authority on the US electric grid and senior official at the North American Electric

Reliability Corp., as saying that these challenges could trigger "cascading blackouts and widespread power interruptions."

Automakers and utilities will be forced to work out these kinks over time. In the meantime, chargers, charging times, and the grid are three good reasons Toyota will stay focused on a hybrid approach. Another reason is because the strategy is working. Many consumers are reluctant to make the switch, so what appeared to be a rush to battery-electric vehicles has stalled dramatically. At the time of this writing, the share of the retail market held by EVs has leveled out at around 9 percent for several months.[10] Hybrid sales, Toyota's strong suit, in the first three quarters of 2023, jumped 48 percent over the prior-year period.[11]

Toyota's hybrid approach sustains revenue today, and it's also fueling innovation. The company has made public its intention to produce a solid-state EV battery capable of running for 900 miles and charging in under ten minutes. It's no coincidence that the company has more than 1,000 patents in solid-state battery research.[12]

Dr. Jane Lubchenco, the deputy director for climate and environment in the White House's Office of Science and Technology Policy, said in 2021, "Every bit of warming matters, and every bit of avoided warming matters."[13] Those who believe in singular strategies like "electrify everything" likely don't appreciate Lubchenco's pragmatism, but she properly points out that an array of solutions—silver buckshot, not a silver bullet—is needed to meet the climate change challenge. With this approach, we use more of the cleanest possible energies available with urgency and in new unique ways.

Can we imagine that it is possible to do a thousand things better than we do them today? Follow me to 2050. In that year, we're going to see thousands of things that will make net zero a reality for our world.

TIME JUMP TO 2050

We have arrived at our destination: 2050. It's a year in which conversations about climate change and the energy transition have shifted in remarkable ways. Two things immediately capture the attention of the climate conscious: First, the planet's temperature has stopped rising and is holding steady at a 1.5 degrees Celsius increase over the pre-industrial average. Second, the concentration of greenhouse gases has not surpassed the CO_2 readings taken at the Mauna Loa Observatory in June 2020—417.1 parts per million—which, at the time, was a record high and caused much alarm.[14]

You might not think this is a statistic to celebrate. Too much CO_2 remains in the atmosphere even in this scenario. In 2050, however, worldwide energy demand has grown substantially, yet CO_2 emissions have not. Better yet, we can now project a decrease of atmospheric CO_2 over the latter half of the twenty-first century.

With its enormous economic influence, the United States led the way in changing the trajectory of the world's climate. America didn't do it alone, however. Every country had to be part of the solution, and countries with much at stake played ambitious and productive roles.

Once one of the most polluted, populous, and economically strained nations in the world, India is thriving in 2050.[15] The country invested dramatically in affordable and accessible solar energy as part of its pledge to reach net zero emissions by 2070.[16]

Even China, who in the 2020s was building more coal-fired electric generation than any other country, has become a clean-energy leader. Beginning in the late 2020s, severe food shortages sparked by climate change created enough political pressure on China's leaders to change course on carbon emissions. (There is precedent for this bit of speculative history. In July 1972, the Soviet Union purchased ten million short tons of grain, mainly wheat and corn, from the United States, representing one-fourth of the US wheat harvest.[17] At the time, no one could have imagined the Soviets and Americans coming to the table to forge any kind of agreement on any matter. As writer and novelist Pearl S. Buck put it, however, "A hungry man can't see right or wrong. He just sees food." Crop shortfalls in 1971 and 1972 forced the Soviet Union to make a deal with a sworn adversary for grain. Unfortunately, crises are sometimes required to achieve real change.)

In our 2050 world, net zero carbon emissions have dropped dramatically thanks in part to China's response to a humanitarian and economic crisis. The country followed through on its 2020 pledge to work toward carbon neutrality by 2060, and as a result, the entire globe benefited.[18]

When we look back on today from this version of 2050, I predict with confidence that we will be astonished by the distance we have traveled. We shouldn't be surprised, though. Through my conversations with an array of energy transition thinkers, I have come to see the outlines of positive change happening right now in the 2020s.

Katharine Hayhoe

February 8, 2020 • Season 3 • Episode 3

IN 2050, we will owe a great deal of thanks to those who did not simply sound the klaxon of doom but, instead, helped us change and gave us hope. The first, most hopeful voice I found among the many people I had the privilege of hosting on *Path to Zero* was Dr. Katharine Hayhoe, a renowned climate scientist and author of *Saving Us: A Climate Scientist's Case for Hope and Healing in a Divided World*.

While pondering the thousand ways in which we will improve the planet on the path to zero, Katharine's focus on relationship building and productive, positive discussion enables all things on the wide path to emerge and become reality.

Katharine and I met during the COVID-19 pandemic when tensions among political powers and neighbors, family, and friends were extremely high. Katharine told me that no matter where she had traveled over the course of the pandemic, she heard the same two questions over and over when speaking on the topic of climate change:

1. "How do I have a conversation about this issue with a family member, a neighbor, a colleague, a coworker, someone I know?" and,

2. "What gives you hope?"

This conversation gave me all the hope in the world for the future.

Tucker: Why do you think that we seem to be more divided than ever on some of these climate change topics?

Dr. Hayhoe: The Pew Foundation has studied this. In the United States now, people are more politically polarized than they have been since the Civil War.[1] And when we're so polarized, we tend to see people who espouse opposing political or ideological views not as fellow citizens of the same nation, but rather as enemies to be defeated. Their gain is our loss, and the opportunity for bipartisanship or for compromise is viewed as weakness rather than strength.

Dr. Hayhoe mentioned the internet and the way it's become a conduit for heated conversations with no real-life consequences for the keyboard warriors behind the screens.

Dr. Hayhoe: When I speak to them in person, the number of [people] willing to actually get up and scream insults into my face . . . I could count on the fingers of one hand in thousands of conversations. But the people who are willing to basically scream insults into my social media feed . . . that number I can count on all the fingers of my hand in just half a day. And that's why I advocate having these in-person conversations with people, because conversations are what bring us together.

Along with climate change being a remarkably polarizing issue, I also see it as an incredibly paralyzing one. A 2022 *New York Times* article described a psychiatrist whose practice is devoted to counseling people who have dread and doom and fear about climate change.[2] A Substack called *Gen Dread* even links thoughts about climate change to suicidal risk.[3]

Tucker: How do you suggest that we negotiate those extremes so we're having more constructive dialogues, and what do you say to people who are just losing hope?

Dr. Hayhoe: We lose hope when we don't think there's anything we can do that will make a difference. Seventy percent of people across the US are already worried about climate change.[4] But half of us—50 percent of us—feel helpless and don't know where to start, and only 8 percent of us would consider ourselves to be activated.

Tucker: How do we bridge the gap between those who are concerned and those who are taking action?

Dr. Hayhoe: By recognizing that there are tangible solutions that every single one of us can engage in. I'm not talking about government policies. I'm not talking about international agreements. And I'm not talking about changing your light bulbs, either. No, I'm talking about something that we don't often realize we have, and that is our voice. It could just be our family that we're talking to, or the people we play golf with or kayak with, or the club that we're part of, or our coworkers.

Tucker: How do we translate those conversations into actions?

Dr. Hayhoe: We can say, "Hey, have we thought about doing an energy audit to save money?" Or, "Have we thought about where we get our electricity from?" Or have we thought about saying, "Hey, it'd be great to have a place for people to plug in their cars since more people are getting electric vehicles these days"? Or, "Hey, what about encouraging people to take public transportation?" Twenty or thirty years ago, often you really couldn't afford to act unless you had money to burn. But these days, it's becoming increasingly possible. So, for example, if an individual wants to get solar panels on their roof, there are credit unions now that will give you a loan where the monthly payment is a hundred dollars below your average power bill over the last year. So that's no longer a luxury.

I confessed to Dr. Hayhoe that, when I looked at what we needed to impact the climate in a positive way, I often felt like there was such a scale, such a magnitude, that it would take all of the world's large corporations to make it happen. I asked her what her thoughts were on the role of existing oil and gas—or even plastics—in the race to improve climate.

Dr. Hayhoe: We are definitely reducing our use of these products. There's no way around it. We can't fix climate change and not reduce it. So, companies are really taking the lead in transitioning a large part of their business model to look at alternative fuels and how to be more efficient with the resources that we do have. We're all humans. We all live on this planet. We all depend on it for everything that we have, the air that we breathe, quite literally, the water we drink, and the food that we eat.

MAGIC WAND

Toward the end of my conversation with Dr. Hayhoe, I asked her the question I pose to every guest on my podcast—which I believe fits perfectly with the topic we have covered in this chapter. Here's the question:

Tucker: This is the only podcast where the guests get a magic wand. I'd like to hand you a magic wand, and I want you to use it to change one thing in the next year that would have the biggest impact regarding climate change, decarbonization, and energy. What would you change or like to see done differently?

Dr. Hayhoe: If I could just wave a magic wand to put a single policy in place, I would put a price on carbon. Because we are already paying that price but in a way that we can't currently see. The idea of pricing carbon is essentially a free-market solution. There's a bipartisan climate solutions caucus in Congress in the Senate, made of half Democrats and half Republicans, who agree on it.

Dr. Hayhoe also named the Climate Leadership Council, which is comprised of many corporations, and even several big oil and gas companies who support pricing carbon.[5] A Canadian herself, Dr. Hayhoe mentioned the fact that Canada has a national price on carbon.[6]

Dr. Hayhoe: But we live in a society now where, again, we see compromise as weakness. We see the other side's loss as our gain. Anything that people could possibly agree on across the aisle seems to immediately fall into that chasm that divides us—that is just getting wider and wider every day. Let's come together on what we can agree on, because there's so much more we agree on than we disagree on, and if we could just work on what we agree on, we could get so much done.

Dr. Hayhoe's most recent book is called *Saving Us* instead of "saving the planet," because saving the planet starts by placing humanity at the center of the conversation.

Dr. Hayhoe: The planet will be orbiting the sun long after we're gone. It really is about saving us, as humans. And we have to do it together or not at all.

WIDENING THE PATH

I hope you were as inspired by my conversation with Dr. Hayhoe as I was. The advice she provides to guide us on our journey to 2050 can be summarized as follows:

- Actively seek out conversations about climate change and global warming. Don't shy away from bringing these questions up with your friends, relatives, and those in your inner circles. If we don't talk about it, nothing will change.

- Spearhead tangible solutions in your community. Do an energy audit with your social club, pool resources to install EV charging stations, and take public transportation when possible.

- Give your friends and families copies of *Saving Us*.

CHAPTER 2

Liquid Energy for Everyone

*Probable impossibilities are to be preferred
to improbable possibilities.*
—ARISTOTLE

In early 2023, BP forecast that the reliance on and therefore the demand for oil and gas would decrease significantly as the energy market adopts more sustainable fuels.[1] A short time later, however, the company reported record sales of petroleum products for 2022 and then stepped away from previous pledges to reduce carbon.[2] BP was not alone. In 2023, both Shell and Exxon also pulled back on plans for cutting carbon emissions in the aftermath of 2022's financial success.[3]

"We cannot justify going for a low return," Shell CEO Wael Sawan said in a media call in February 2023.[4] "Our shareholders deserve to see us going after strong returns. If we cannot achieve the double-digit returns in a business, we need to question very hard whether we should continue in that business. Absolutely, we want to continue to go for lower and lower and lower carbon, but it has to be profitable."

Can companies like BP, Exxon, and Shell continue to invest in hydrocarbon production and make a transition to cleaner fuels that will ultimately get us to net zero? My belief is that these companies want to remain at the forefront of the energy transition and, therefore, not only can do so, but will do so. Their profitability today—if they invest strategically—will fund their profitability of the future.

One of my guests, Tisha Schuller, has an expression: "say yes to both."[5] Hydrocarbon leaders today don't have to abandon their most lucrative product. They can say yes to revenue and yes to investments in the future—alternative fuels that will achieve the net zero reality we need. They can, and must, play both a short and a long game. They can harness the power of today's profits *and* use those profits to invest in a more sustainable future.

Achieving net zero is a challenge of such magnitude that it will require the participation of large companies with access to capital, employees, and distribution. The energy transition is a global-scale challenge, so we need global-scale companies to be part of the solution. We cannot achieve a net zero future without them. To be relevant in the future, they have to think about the day when petroleum reserves run thin.

Saudi Aramco makes a good case study.[6]

Saudi Aramco is now more valuable than the next ten largest energy companies combined. Last year it pulled down $161 billion in profits. Today, the company is, by all measures, performing well, but tomorrow is uncertain. Exactly how much oil remains under the sand in Persian Gulf countries is a closely guarded secret. The expectation is, however, that Bahrain is likely to run out of oil within the decade, Oman in two decades, and the Kingdom by the end of the century, possibly sooner.[7]

TIME JUMP TO 2050

We're in the year 2050 again, looking back in time. When it comes to the energy transition, the history books (prediction: history books will still exist!) talk about the 2020s as the decade when the journey to net zero began in earnest. Carbon intensity—a measure of how clean our electricity is by how many grams of carbon dioxide are released to produce a kilowatt hour (kWh) of electricity—became the best measure of progress, and when that happened, the floodgates of innovation opened for renewable liquid fuels.

Many assumed the clean-energy transition was to be an evolution from liquids and gases to solids, or, put another way, that we would be replacing oil with batteries made of minerals like lithium, cobalt, and nickel. That assumption turned out to be wrong. Despite widespread criticism of liquid fuels and a push to eliminate them, we achieved net zero by investing in a variety of liquid fuels.

In an ironic twist of fate, it was a new table published by the California Air Resources Board (CARB)—an early leader in electrify-everything conversations—that paved the way. The Low Carbon Fuel Standards Pathway Certified Carbon Intensities report showed the remarkable opportunities ahead.[8] Just a few examples from that report comparing the carbon intensity of liquid fuels made in 2023 are shown below. A negative carbon-intensity number means the fuel takes more carbon out of the environment than it produces.

- Dairy Manure Biogas to Electricity   -762.09
- Food Scraps to Compressed Natural Gas   -79.91
- Landfill Gas to Hydrogen   -12.65
- Solar or Wind to Electricity   0.00*
- Used Cooking Oil to Biodiesel   8.63
- Corn Stover to Ethanol   21.58
- Used Cooking Oil to Jet Fuel   26.05
- Organic Waste to Propane   33.00
- Sugarcane Molasses to Ethanol   40.84
- Soybeans to Biodiesel   50.85
- California Grid Electricity   81.49**
- CA Grid Electricity to Hydrogen   164.46

* CARB does not calculate the carbon intensity of the manufacturing, installation, or decommissioning of solar panels or wind turbines.

** Why is grid electricity in California higher in carbon intensity than many liquid fuel products? The California grid was mainly energized by natural gas and (in 2023) was still powered to a smaller extent by coal.[9]

Trillium, a transportation fuels producer in Houston, Texas, put the above numbers in more perspective. Their data showed the carbon intensity of conventional diesel to be 100.[10] Gasoline is very close to the same number. Renewable natural gas converted from dairy waste is remarkably low, at -283.27. In my own industry, by 2050, we saw renewable propane beginning to be produced at scale at a carbon intensity score of 20.50 without blending.

In all, the CARB report detailed more than 1,700 examples of low carbon intensity liquid fuels. The substantive point is that anything below 100 was an improvement, and many kinds of low carbon intensity fuels using many types of manufacturing methods were already in place in 2023. In 2050, the innovation gains in liquid fuel carbon intensity mean that dozens of formerly high carbon applications—shipping, trucking, generators—are all fueled by low to negative carbon intensive fuels. Let's warp back to 2022 and talk more about how liquid fuels created a "clean energy everywhere" future.

Kevin Lucke

July 23, 2022 • Season 3 • Episode 17

RENEWABLES AREN'T confined to solar and wind like many people think. Renewable fuels provide us an immediate reduction of emissions that the "electrify everything" route cannot match. Some are known as "drop in" fuels, meaning there is no need for reengineering of the engines being powered. A propane generator, for example, runs just as well on renewable propane as it does on conventional propane. Synthetic aviation fuel (SAF) is another kind of drop-in fuel. It is typically a blend of 50 percent conventional jet fuel with fuel made from recovered waste products (fats, oils, and greases or forest residues), requiring no aircraft engine modifications. It makes a difference too. Airbus claims the SAF it uses can reduce lifecycle CO_2 emissions by up to 80 percent compared to conventional fuel.[1]

The same isn't perfectly true for biodiesel fuel. It is not chemically the same as its conventional counterpart, so most engines cannot run on pure biodiesel without modification. In blended form, however, it's a much cleaner alternative to regular diesel fuel. The good news about all these renewables is that the pace of innovation taking place in liquid fuels is truly remarkable.

Here are two *Path to Zero* interviews that will leave you encouraged that large oil and gas companies, and exceptionally innovative startup companies, are indeed making big investments in the clean energy future.

In this conversation with Kevin Lucke, the president of Chevron Renewable Energy Group, we discussed renewable fuels and the fight against climate change with renewable energy.[2] Kevin made a very important point—that it was going to "take all forms of energy to meet the growing demand of society."

I agree. People really don't understand the benefits of renewable fuels, nor do they understand the vast reach of liquid fuels—particularly diesel and gasoline, and, for that reason, this was an illuminating interview.

Tucker: For me, someone who has watched these fats, oils, and greases transform into energy and really understands the carbon intensity, it's an easy answer. But I'm often shocked at people who say there's just no future.

Kevin: What's really neat about both biodiesel and renewable diesel is that they can be dropped into existing equipment today and [begin] lowering our carbon.

Tucker: As someone who works not only with end customers but also with manufacturers, I see the concept of a drop-in fuel as critical to rapid acceleration of the technology.

Kevin: You just can't flip a switch and make the change. Getting solutions that are shovel-ready today to start the transition is really what we're trying to achieve. Chevron has made a commitment to produce 100,000 barrels a day by 2030. The Renewable Energy Group now has about a third of the capacity to reach that goal.

I think the future is exciting, Tucker, but it's going to take all of us to make a difference. And when I say all of us, it means all the different forms of renewable fuels that are out there. We can't pick one and say that's the solution.

Tucker: How important is carbon intensity to your business?

Kevin: Our customers have sustainability officers who are highly educated, so carbon intensity is a big part of the value proposition, and this has clearly changed in the past five years. The fact that the fuels are produced locally makes this a win all the way around.

I asked Kevin to look into the future at other ways of lowering carbon. He is excited about renewable diesel. When talking about it, he educated me about FOGs—fats, oils, and greases.

Examples of these FOGs include soybean oil, animal fats, vegetable oils, and even recycled cooking oil.[3] While chemically similar to traditional diesel fuel, FOG-based diesel is produced from non–crude oil sources, making it a lower carbon intensity option, earning it the name "green diesel." A major benefit is reduced tailpipe emissions.[4] It can also be blended with traditional diesel, creating a lower-carbon product, and renewable diesel has applications in areas such as powering ships, cars, heavy-duty vehicles, and high-speed trains.

Just before Kevin and I met for his interview, I happened to be at LAX in the United terminal. I saw a banner that read, "Every airplane leaving this terminal uses sustainable fuel." Sustainable aviation fuel (SAF) is made from biomass and is a renewable and low-carbon alternative to conventional fossil-based jet fuel.[5] It is produced from organic materials, such as corn grain; oil seeds; algae; other fats, oils, and greases; agricultural residues; forestry residues; wood-mill waste; city solid-waste streams; wet wastes (like manures); and dedicated energy crops. It's an important liquid fuel for the future because aviation accounts for 2 percent of all human-caused carbon dioxide (CO_2) emissions and 12 percent of all transportation CO_2 emissions.

When I mentioned that story to Kevin, he wasn't surprised.

Kevin: The airlines have made public commitments that they

46

are going to make changes in the way they operate, and sustainable aviation fuels is one of those ways. We have a lot of work going on in the feedstock space, looking at alternative feedstocks. The most exciting space is in the feedstock area.

This is where products like renewable natural gas (RNG) come into the liquid fuels arena. RNG is created from methane capture from wastewater, landfills, animal excrement, and agricultural residue, such as crop residues, methane digesters, and food waste.[6] It can be used to replace conventional natural gas and is growing in popularity due to the environmental and economic benefits it provides. It emits significantly fewer greenhouse gases than conventional sources, which makes it an excellent source of renewable fuel in the short-term.

Tucker: Renewable propane also should be mentioned here, and I am convinced there is no better liquid fuel on the planet today.

Kevin: We are continuing to sell that to the transportation fuel market, and we are expanding our plant in Louisiana. We are going to need all sources of lower-carbon solutions, and renewable propane is certainly one of those going into the future.

Renewable propane produces a lot of energy for scores of purposes and millions of people with virtually zero particulate

47

matter, zero impact to the ozone, zero toxicity, and zero potential for storage-related contamination. There are more than eleven ways to make renewable propane, but perhaps most interesting and in the context of Kevin's remarks about innovative feedstocks is the manufacturing of it using a plant called *Camelina sativa*. This leads right into a fantastic conversation I had with Richard Palmer, the CEO of another important company called Global Clean Energy.[7] Richard and his team are camelina experts and are the only vertically integrated renewable-fuels operation in the United States, mimicking the models of the majors, with highly optimized upstream, midstream, and downstream operations.

Richard Palmer

February 15, 2023 • Season 4 • Episode 14

IN THE MUSTARD seed family, *Camelina sativa* is an oilseed crop that is a non-food cousin of canola. Its seeds can be converted into renewable propane and used as a drop-in fuel for any existing application. The variety of liquid fuels camelina produces may soon have the lowest carbon intensity score of any plant feedstock, and as you'll see, it brings a variety of other benefits to the sustainability conversation.

Richard and I started with the big picture regarding carbon intensity.

Richard: Everything that you do in that entire supply chain goes into the carbon intensity of the finished renewable fuel. In ours, the upstream is an agricultural product above the ground to produce the feedstock of the renewable fuel. In the midstream, we aggregate the crop, clean it, do some pre-processing to it, then transport it to where it is going to be turned into fuel.

49

Downstream, we process it into finished product, primarily renewable diesel, renewable propane, renewable naphtha, and renewable butane.

Camelina grows on land that would otherwise be fallow or idle and requires very little water to thrive. In addition, it does not displace food crops and matures in less than one hundred days. This wonderful little plant is also resistant to insect pests and diseases and offers pollination opportunities that benefit bees and promote biodiversity.

Richard: Today, Global Clean Energy has the largest portfolio of patents on camelina and all the domestic and international regulatory approvals. It's always about the feedstock. We have been hyper-focused on not using a food-grade product to produce the fuels we do.

Tucker: Why is non-food-grade an important attribute?

Richard: The expansion of the renewable-fuels market is highly dependent on feedstock availability. Eighty-five percent of the costs and 100 percent of the carbon footprint are determined by that feedstock. Feedstocks are the building blocks of renewable fuels, which are mostly sourced from food products. Ethanol is primarily sourced from corn or sugar, while renewable diesel and biodiesel is sourced from soybeans, canola, or tallow. This concerns regulators and users, as it has a direct impact on food security—not just availability of it but the price of it. Camelina is scalable as a non-food renewable feedstock, and all we need is large commercial adoption.

The sustainability attributes are even more impressive when you look at camelina from a farmer's perspective. When Richard and I talked about the viewpoint of farmers, he opened a whole new view of what sustainability, when done beautifully, generates.

Richard: Farmers generally have a primary crop—a wheat farmer, a corn farmer, a soybean farmer. When they are not growing their crop, [the land is fallow]. Some farmers put a cover crop on fallow land to protect [it] from erosion, and it costs them to keep that cover crop in [and] they don't harvest it. It gets tilled under or sprayed down and killed, or it just dies naturally. Camelina protects like a cover crop, but it pays like a cash crop. It has very quick maturity between crop cycles. It also captures carbon above and below the ground while it's growing. Farmers use existing equipment to harvest the crop, so they don't have to invest in any more equipment. We're saying plant our crop instead of no crop. When they have no crop on their land, it costs them money. It is a very easy feedstock to convert into a renewable fuel. What's left over from the processing is a high-protein biomass, which is used as animal feed. This takes pressure off of soy meal or canola meal or other food crops.

Global Clean Energy bought an old Shell refinery in Bakersfield a few years ago and has upgraded the site in the middle of the highest demand market for renewable fuels: California.[1] That makes transport of the fuel shorter, but there's more. The design of the plant has its own sustainability features.

Richard: When you use a vegetable oil in a refinery, it gives off a lot of extra heat. That heat can be used in other processes within the refinery, so we have less fossil fuel that has to be burned. So rather than using a new source, we use the direct heat from the process to reduce the amount of energy and carbon intensity of the process. That's beneficial for everybody.

Tucker: When you start talking about a product with a carbon intensity as low as seven produced in the location where it will be used, you have an affordable, resilient, and environmentally beneficial product that's arguably the best choice for transportation right now.

Richard: We have very good line of sight to a sub-zero carbon intensity for our finished goods. We can offset a lot of fossil fuel use with renewable fuels.

Tucker: But is there a place for liquid fuels, or is the future only electric?

Richard: When you see a bumper sticker on an electric car that says zero emissions, that isn't where the emissions are created. You have to see what the source of the electricity is that's charging that vehicle. All of the electricity is not renewable. The majority is not. Electric requires an enormous amount of infrastructure upgrades. Electricity is not portable; you don't put it in a can to ship it. It's going to take quite a bit of time to get to that. Renewable liquid fuels are here now. You can grow it sustainably, and there are drop-in replacements here now that can have a huge impact on the environment. We can do electric as a portion of it, liquid fuels as a portion of it. It's not just one solution. There are trillions of dollars of infrastructure already built for liquid fuels in the vehicle, and the entire supply chain that supplies those vehicles around the world, so to think that it would all of a sudden just be gone quickly in any of our lifetimes is just fallacy. And, we have the ability to be below zero carbon intensity, not just at zero.

Wow! When I listen to Richard and Kevin, two brilliant leaders in today's energy space, talk about the future of zero carbon or below liquid fuels, I can't help but be encouraged about the possibilities ahead. It's going to take more of this thinking, and our elected officials' awareness, to accelerate adoption of renewable liquid fuels.

Kevin: I believe those groups of public policymakers really still play a critical part in the success of the renewable fuels industry, and, so, having lawmakers willing to incentivize the use of lower-carbon alternatives is critical to our success. We do believe that lawmakers have a stronger understanding of the importance of lower carbon alternatives and the positive benefits that they have for our planet, but we still need to educate them in this space.

MAGIC WANDS

Like I do with all my *Path to Zero* guests, I granted Kevin and Richard the use of a magic wand, with some guidance.

Tucker: Here's how you use that wand. You get to wave it one time to change one thing in the next year that will have the biggest impact regarding climate, decarbonization, and energy. How would you use that wand?

Kevin: I'm going to use that wand to make a wish that every person on Earth has an understanding of the benefits of biofuels and the use of lower-carbon solutions. And as we discussed, it really includes our elected officials to be supportive of policies for lower carbon into the future.

Richard: I am going to use my wand in a *Wizard of Oz* context. When I wave my magic wand, I would give everybody a big brain, a big heart, and a lot of courage. I think that would really drive a lot of change. People would step up, look at the logic of things, and have the courage to drive for it.

Is there really a future for liquid fuels, and can they deliver on our quest for zero-or-better carbon intensity? What Kevin and Richard taught us in their interviews is that electrification isn't the only solution to climate change. I enjoyed those conversations so much because they are "yes to both" thinkers.

WIDENING THE PATH

Net zero won't happen unless we focus on energy diversification, and low-carbon liquid fuels give us an enormous leg up in the race against climate change. The discussions with Kevin Lucke and Richard Palmer reminded me just how much we are counting on so many people to get there. Here are a few things we can all do:

If you're concerned about curbing climate change, be open to a variety of solutions. Liquid fuels with low carbon intensity are available today and can reduce carbon emissions now.

Be encouraged! Innovation is happening in ways that we could never have imagined. Camelina, for example, as the feedstock for renewable propane, came onto the scene just a few years ago.

Make renewable liquid fuels a part of your own climate change advocacy. If you have an opportunity to talk to elected officials about the subject, share your knowledge of these highly flexible and portable alternatives.

CHAPTER 3

From ESG to 3-D

I do have reasons for hope: our clever brains,
the resilience of nature, the indomitable human spirit,
and above all, the commitment of young people
when they're empowered to take action.
—JANE GOODALL

Your grandparents may have told you they hiked to school uphill both ways during snowstorms, but you may be telling your grandchildren about the challenge of sleeping through sweat-soaked sheets with the air conditioner running wide open.

In a recent lifestyle article for AccuWeather, CNN reporter Sandee LaMotte gave ten tips for sleeping in the heat.[1] She began the article by asking her readers if they are waking up in "puddles of sweat," if they're even able to sleep. "That's the grim reality for millions of people around the globe suffering through severe, unbearable heat waves," she continued.

LaMotte referenced a study that shows that incidences of "dangerous heat—defined as 103 degrees Fahrenheit (39.4 degrees Celsius)—will more than double by 2050 in the midlatitude regions, which include Western Europe and countries such as China, Japan, and the United States."[2] And there will be no relief at night. "Nights are warming faster than days on average in most of the US, the 2018 National Climate Assessment found," she continued.[3] "That's dangerous for sleep—a vital period when the body and brain do house-keeping chores such as repairing and discarding old cells and generating new ones."

The 2023 National Climate Assessment does nothing to make us more comfortable.[4] A pull-out graphic from that report reads, "Global temperature has increased faster in the past 50 years than at any time in at least the past 2,000 years."

WEATHER EXTREMES

Dangerous heat is just one example of a weather-extreme future that will push people, and our current electrical grid, to the brink. Severe storms are yet another. These are names that folks won't soon forget:

Hurricane Bertha made landfall in Charleston. Cristobal hit Puerto Rico and Louisiana.[5] Fay made it all the way to New Jersey. Harvey wreaked havoc through Texas. Isaias churned its way up the East Coast of the United States. While the world was suffering tragic and unprecedented challenges during the height of the COVID-19 pandemic, extreme weather didn't let up. These tropical storms and hurricanes made for a record-breaking 2020 Atlantic hurricane season, with thirty named storms—eleven of which made landfall in the United States.[6] Hurricane season has posed an increasingly serious threat to public safety, as these storms are devastating wherever they land.

Not only did these storms increase in intensity and severity, but they also impacted communities previously untouched by such disasters.[7] Go back in time just a bit: in October 2012, Superstorm Sandy swept the Eastern Seaboard all the way up to New England—a population that was shocked by the effects of the event even though it had time to prepare. The residents of Milford, Connecticut, for example, found themselves struggling in the aftermath of this major storm.[8] Extensive damage to the electric grid meant no working pumps for water, no refrigeration, and no way to charge phones. Miles of tangled transmission lines and uprooted wooden utility poles served notice that it would take days or weeks for power to be restored.

Milford wasn't alone then and isn't alone now. Nearly everyone in the country relies on the electric grid for power to keep the lights on and their lives running. Extreme weather events—derecho winds, flooding, tornados, wildfires, and hurricanes—repeatedly expose the nearly six million miles of power lines and wooden poles of our aging US electric grid to significant risk.[9] While the East Coast suffered through the 2020 hurricane season, California gave us an example of how susceptible the electric grid is to failure when high temperatures across the West resulted in power outages affecting more than three million people.[10]

The Inflation Reduction Act was enacted into federal policy in 2022. The act allocated $7.5 billion in tax credits to incentivize the installation of more EV charging stations.[11] Passage of that law didn't fix the grid though. It created an ESG—and not in the environmental, social, and governance sense. My version of ESG stands for "electricity supply gap." It is this gap that sits between us and sustained progress on carbon emission reductions. It is this same gap that puts grid reliability at serious risk.

Electric grid reliability and resiliency issues aren't new. In 2018, the Department of Energy reported that 70 percent of the country's transformers and transmission power lines were at least twenty-five years old, while 60 percent of circuit breakers were at least thirty years old.[12] What is new is the precipitous decline in the power generation capability of the entire system.

PJM Interconnection, the grid operator in thirteen northeast states providing power to sixty-five million Americans, raised the alarm on this subject in 2023.[13] For that year, it forecast a large decline in power generation as coal and natural gas plants were being forced to close due to federal agency requirements and ESG (environment, social, and governance) commitments at a quicker pace than new or intermittent generation could be built. The calculations showed that over 20 percent of PJM's current generation capacity—enough to light up thirty million households—was at risk of retiring by 2030.

The Department of Energy believes a solution to our ESG problem is to build more high-voltage transmission lines so different regions of the country can share power when demand surges.[14] That concept comes with a price tag of several trillion dollars by mid-century, though, and local opposition to landscape-changing projects—high voltage transmission lines included—remains seriously challenging.[15]

RESILIENCY AWARENESS

The hoarding behavior we witnessed at the beginning of COVID-19 raised awareness that humans don't generally prepare very well for extended power outages.[16] Most homes are equipped with little more than flashlights and batteries and maybe a few candles.

Relatively few have an alternative power source for critical appliances like refrigerators, which is a big problem, since food and many medicines spoil quickly. A typical refrigerator, for example, if kept closed, can protect food for about four hours without power. A half-full freezer can do the same for about twenty-four hours. It's good to be aware of these vulnerabilities, because it leads to brainstorming ways to reduce exposure. Resiliency thinking, however, requires an understanding of the strengths and weaknesses of various energy sources.

Contrary to popular belief, solar panels alone don't keep electricity flowing when the grid goes down. Thousands of homes and businesses in New York and New Jersey learned this the hard way during extended blackouts following superstorm Sandy. When interviewed back then by the *New York Times*, Queens resident Ed Antonio lamented that his forty-two-panel, $70,000 solar system went unused for almost a month.[17] The same was true for his neighbors who had rooftop solar. "That's a lot of power sitting, just sitting," he said. Unless paired with batteries, solar panels typically feed directly into the grid during the day and pull power back to run the house at night. No stored power stays in the panels or the lines. California's love affair with solar is likely to cool off as the state realizes its limitations. During the 2020 blackouts, the governor talked about how the shift to renewables had created gaps in the state's energy supply, acknowledging, "We cannot sacrifice reliability."[18]

Other, more astronomical (pun intended) challenges affect solar power production as well. On October 14, 2023, shortly after 9:00 a.m., the sun went dark from Oregon through Nevada, Utah, New Mexico, and all the way to the Texas Gulf. The so-called "ring-of-fire"solar eclipse cut the output of more than one hundred solar power plants across the country, resulting in 14,500 megawatts of solar power idled in California for several hours and 11,900 megawatts in Texas.[19] In all, the nation lost an estimated 28,300 gigawatts of power.

How do we compensate for intermittency? Diesel generators can provide power when needed, but, in the wake of a devastating storm, they can't run for long periods before fuel runs out. They also come with several significant downsides: They're noisy. They emit criteria pollutants—ozone, nitrogen dioxide, sulfur dioxide, carbon monoxide, and especially particulate matter, or soot. Diesel fuel itself oxidizes in the tank in as little as thirty days, rendering the generator powerless and requiring the fuel to be dumped.

Gasoline doesn't provide long-term confidence either. Pumps at gas stations don't work during a blackout because they depend on electricity to function. Even if they do work, supplies are quickly exhausted if roads are impassable for tanker trucks. Some of the most iconic pictures following Sandy showed miles-long lines at gas stations with customers being turned away when supplies ran out. In 2017, following Hurricane Harvey's landfall near Corpus Christi, long lines for gasoline formed as far away as San Antonio, Austin, and Dallas due to refinery shutdowns.[20]

It wouldn't be wrong to think that wood-burning fireplaces or stoves can provide some resiliency during long-term power outages. Assuming space is available, properly dried firewood can be stockpiled, and professionally installed fireplaces can certainly provide warmth to a home. On the downside, unless you've got the right equipment and utensils, it's not easy to cook over a wood fire, and the environmental issues are obvious. Burning wood eliminates carbon-consuming trees and puts a lot of soot and CO_2 into the air—none of which is good.

What energy alternatives exist that can overcome the downsides of diesel or gas generators, the implausibility of wood, and the limitations of solar? Propane checks a lot of the boxes.

Propane, especially renewable propane, is a clean, low-emissions, resilient energy choice capable of delivering efficient, on-site energy during power outages. Propane-powered appliances like fireplaces, stoves, ovens, and generators are safe and easy to operate. Storage is flexible as well. Cylinders or tanks come in a range of sizes suitable to a home or business and require no additional grid-powered pumps to operate. On-site storage can sustain occupants for weeks or months, and when it's time to resupply, it can be replenished via retail stores or delivered by trucks small enough to navigate storm-damaged roads.

A NEW DEFINITION OF ESG

Now, propane is not a perfect energy, because a perfect energy doesn't exist. What propane allows us to see, however, is that our grid is a single point of failure. We need multiple options—our silver buckshot of a thousand ways, if you will—to keep the lights on, water pumps flowing, medical equipment working, and refrigerators cooling. In short, we need to recognize and respond to our new ESG—the electricity supply gap.

Some advocates believe the one solution to achieving net zero carbon emissions is to go all in on electric. It makes sense if you don't look behind the plug. As we've discussed, the projected cost for an "electrify everything" future is $25 to $35 trillion for the United States alone, and that is only for the transmission infrastructure.[21] Not only will this solution require an exorbitant amount of money to install, but making this future a reality will also require massive marketing campaigns to win over the public who will be paying for it. Transitioning to an electric-only world is financially impractical, does nothing to solve the energy source decarbonization problem, and does not solve the single point of failure problem that is our grid.

REIMAGINING THE GRID

When stranded on Mars in the movie *The Martian*, Matt Damon's character, Mark Watney, confronted with an array of life-or-death choices, says[22] to his video diary, "In the face of overwhelming odds, I am left with only one option: I'm going to have to science the s*** out of this." That's a great line, isn't it? That's what we need to do. We are inside a global-scale energy-transformation flex point where innovation of every sort, all aimed in the same direction toward a net zero carbon future, is essential.

We need to re-imagine the grid in a way that makes more electrification possible and won't mean rolling blackouts or waking up in swimming pools of perspiration. The better solution to the electricity supply gap and fragile grid is a wide path of energy solutions. That is exactly how our 2050 world will operate.

TIME JUMP TO 2050

Our 2050 world operates on what I call a 3-D grid. It's a bulwark of new and better overhead lines, reinforced underground pipelines, and, in the middle, multi-use, portable liquid fuels.

The 2021 ransomware attack that shut down the Colonial Pipeline—a Texas-to-New-Jersey conveyor of 2.5 million barrels a day of diesel, gasoline, and jet fuel—was a wakeup call for why an expanded view of our nation's energy grid needed to be taken seriously.[23]

DarkSide, the cybercriminal syndicate that perpetrated the attack, managed to pull off the largest global disruption of energy distribution since Saudi Arabian oil supplies were attacked with drones in 2019.[24] The Colonial Pipeline attack was the second major disruption of the US energy system in 2021, following winter storm Uri's bludgeoning of the Texas electric grid in February of that year.

As with Uri, the Colonial hack created enormous uncertainty and chaos, stalling crude oil refining and spiking energy prices. In the name of decarbonization, cities around the country had begun adopting all-electrification building codes, but a homogenous power system presented a giant, nearly irresistible target to both volatile weather and web-based criminals. Like the body's own highly diversified immune system, energy diversity made possible by climate-friendly energy solutions created resilience in the face of continuous attack.

A 3-D GRID

Decision-makers quickly realized that when overhead power lines could be taken down by extreme weather and underground pipes could be shut down by hackers, it was time for a new catastrophe-resistant approach to take center stage. And that is exactly what we were able to do by 2050. How did we accomplish it? We decentralized and diversified.

Decentralization of the grid started with investments in microgrids. Microgrids are attachable to main grids when necessary and supported by site-storable energy. Batteries as energy-storing devices weren't the answer; they are just as hackable as the Colonial Pipeline. Malware could easily brick a computer-controlled battery system by tricking it to overcharge.[25] So, an elegant solution called Power-to-X came into its own. Power-to-X is the conversion of renewably sourced electricity into zero-or-better carbon intensity liquid fuels.[26] The advantages of easy storability and transportability helped us recognize liquid fuels as better batteries.

By the late 2020s, we had all the components of a 3-D grid. Industrial-scale wind and solar costs had fallen, while their electric generation capacity continued to rise. At the same time, we were able to convert pipelines to carry hydrogen and novel liquid fuels like renewable propane, green ammonia, and dimethyl ether. This combination proved affordable and terrifically resilient in the face of increasingly severe weather events, political instability around the world, and more aggressive cyber criminals. What started as an electricity supply gap transitioned to a better conversation about our collective Energy Security Gap.

Jeffrey Schlegelmilch
August 1, 2022 • Season 3 • Episode 13

IS THE 2050 vision of a 3-D grid plausible? In August 2022, I tested the idea with Jeffrey Schlegelmilch, a research scholar, the director of the National Center for Disaster Preparedness at Columbia University's Earth Institute, and the author of *Rethinking Readiness: A Brief Guide to Twenty-First-Century Megadisasters.*[1] In this eye-opening interview, Jeffrey and I discussed climate disaster preparedness and the ultimate goal of decarbonizing the grid for a cleaner, more sustainable future.

We began our conversation by discussing how carbon pollution is responsible for the increase in frequency and severity of climate disasters. It's no secret that wildfires are burning longer, extreme heat is getting hotter, drought conditions are persisting longer, and hurricanes are becoming more intense. Scientists predict that these phenomena will only get worse.

Tucker: We know increasingly severe weather is coming. How can we prepare?

Jeffrey: Unfortunately, I'd say it's a very data-rich time when it comes to disasters because we're experiencing so many. But, also, the silver linings are that there's a lot of opportunity to translate that into ways to better our readiness and better the outcomes for everyone in our communities.

Leading up to this interview, I had spent time poring over data myself. I was shocked by the changing frequency. If you go back twenty years, severe weather events like hurricanes, fires, and floods occurred six hundred to eight hundred times per year. In 2022, these events were happening more like 25,000 times per year.

Tucker: Is this data consistent with your findings?

Jeffrey: We're seeing more disasters and we're seeing it for a variety of reasons.

Jeffrey said that he is often asked if we're actually seeing more disasters or if it simply appears that way since we have more infrastructure and more expensive areas in the pathway of disasters, as compared to the past. Or is it both?

Jeffrey: We're seeing more. We're seeing the impacts of climate change. We're seeing the impacts of development in a very aggressive and expansive way, and so it's enhancing the vulnerability to disasters.

He went on to say that, at the same time, we're also seeing an increase in the hazards that lead to disasters. One of the primary subjects he addresses in his book, *Rethinking Readiness*, is how development is actually contributing to these increasing threats and vulnerabilities.

Jeffrey: To end on a slightly positive note on this comment, if we are contributing to the threat and vulnerability, it means that we can also take actions to reduce the threats and the vulnerabilities. It's within our control to have more positive outcomes.

Tucker: Humans are pretty good at responding to crises. We're not as good at preventing them. We tend to think more about FEMA-style recovery than preparedness. How far have we come in terms of disaster response and preparation, and where can we improve?

Jeffrey: Certainly, if you look at metrics of lives lost as a result of disasters, you actually see, even with an increase in disasters, the relative number of lives lost seems to be decreasing. But we're really not good at getting folks back on their feet. We're better in areas that are highly visible.

He gave the example of New Orleans and Bourbon Street, a tourist area, versus the Lower Ninth Ward, a low-income area left beleaguered for much longer than the highly visible areas after Hurricane Katrina.

Jeffrey: It's a very uneven experience. I think it's something where we can all get in a room with any group of people and agree very quickly that preparedness saves. Dollars spent in preparedness saves. I think we have trouble making it very relevant before the disaster strikes. After the disaster, you have buildings down, you have trees down; it's very visual. Preparedness is more abstract, there's more uncertainty, and it's tougher to wrap our heads around that and to take decisive actions.

Tucker: I'm a civil engineer by training. Do you believe today's building codes and standards are keeping pace with resiliency needs? Are we building in the right places and with the right technologies, or do we need to make rapid changes in flood maps and building codes?

Jeffrey: I should note that building codes have been incredibly important in averting losses of lives from disasters, ranging from more significant things like hurricanes to small-scale things like a house fire, which is a global-shifting disaster for the individuals involved. The challenge is that, as we're seeing more and more of these changes and more and more of this damage, the changes that need to be made are greater and greater to avert the kind of damage that we're going to see. For many people, their biggest asset is their home, and all of a sudden that loses value or becomes more expensive because the insurance has shot up X percent as a result of this. So, the process of defining these flood maps is not wholly objective and scientific.

Tucker: So, it's not easy to make rapid changes because of the human considerations involved.

Jeffrey: There are a lot of politics involved, and there are a lot of social ramifications involved. On the one hand, it slows the process, which means we have more and more places sitting in harm's way because we're not making the changes we need to make. At the same time, by making these changes, we're also upsetting social ecosystems, economic ecosystems at the same time, and that's very immediate and has very significant repercussions. So, it's a very, very difficult problem, but one that's only going to get harder the more that that can is kicked down the road.

I wanted to get Jeffrey's interpretation of electric grid resiliency, especially when regarding preparedness equity, a front-of-mind topic for me. At its core, achieving net zero is a human rights issue. In order to get behind the massive changes that will have to take place to meet our 2050 net zero goal, we must have a perspective outside ourselves—a viewpoint that is about bettering a world many of us may never see.

Tucker: Do you believe, in the context of disaster preparedness, that equity is important?

Jeffrey: There are certain lifelines that cut across communities and facilitate civil society. They make modern life possible—roads, fuel, and energy, including the electric grid. So, we can look at the electric grid as a circuit, and it's bound by the laws of physics and engineered, but that circuit is overlaid on a community. I live in New York. I give this example: [in] a wealthy area like the Upper West Side, a blackout for ten thousand customers for two days has a certain impact. You go to another part of the city, say the South Bronx, an area with lower socioeconomic status and more health problems, and you have the same outage, ten thousand people for two days, it's a very different impact. You're likely to see more health impacts, more disruptions to households.

He went on to explain that the inability for certain communities to cope with disaster has roots in history and policy.

Jeffrey: We can go back and look at the legacies of redlining[2] from a hundred years ago and how wealth was accumulated and denied and how, to this day, you can see disparities of infrastructure investments and all sorts of things that can predict worse outcomes in disasters. And, unfortunately, we saw this in the COVID-19 pandemic, too, in terms of where the burden was and where the immediate access was to testing and vaccines and things like that. When we look at the value of investments that can build resilience, we also fail to see that, actually, by reframing how we position some of these investments, there can actually be a much greater benefit to civil society just by putting some of these investments where they're needed most and where they'll mitigate against some of the most severe outcomes of a disaster.

I couldn't agree more. When we begin to see the pursuit of net zero as a catalyst for serving other human beings, it's easy to get excited. And like the liquid fuels in the previous chapter, there's even more to talk about.

The nation's power grid is under stress like never before.[3] Heat waves over past summers have pushed the power grid to its limits, but new energy supplies, including renewables, are helping it survive.[4] I asked Jeffrey how concerned he was about the grid's ability to withstand the weather shocks that were sure to come.

Jeffrey: On a scale of one to ten, I guess I would say a seven or eight in the near term, and in the longer term, we are seeing a lot of investments being made. I think that this is one of the areas where we may potentially see more progress in a shorter period of time. I hope to see more hardening of the grid, more resilience for the grid, more integration of technologies that allow for rerouting of power, for detection of outages, and deployment of microgrids.

That comment opens the door to yet another great *Path to Zero* conversation.

Michael Burr

December 1, 2020 • Season 2 • Episode 2

ENTER MICHAEL BURR, founder of the Microgrid Institute and the Microgrid Finance Group and chief editor of over twenty volumes of energy industry journals. Michael started our conversation by helping me understand the basics of what a microgrid is and how it works.

Michael: A microgrid basically is an independent energy system, or a system that's capable of operating independently from the larger grid if it's indeed connected to a utility grid. It can just be simply a part of the larger grid that's operated as an island, a safe power island. In some cases, it's still a literal island. It'll be literally in the ocean, or it'll be in a remote community someplace where there is no utility service or where the service is just very, very limited.

Solar and wind are the most common forms of renewable

energy for a microgrid, but it's also possible to have hydro-electric or even geothermal sources powering an independent grid. I asked Michael why this arena was attracting interest, and his response pulled the ESG—energy security gap—into the spotlight.

Michael: Today, most people are looking for energy independence. And if you want energy independence, then you want a fuel that doesn't require delivery from outside, to the degree that that's possible. So, one of the things that really is a good marriage of technologies is the advance in photovoltaics, in particular, as well as batteries that make it possible for people to use solar energy in an independently operating system in a microgrid. All of the microgrids that we're working on these days do include some component of renewable energy. The technology is starting to change the market. It's making it possible to provide services that customers need and that they can't get from the traditional utility industry—or they weren't, anyway, and haven't been getting from an industry that was built around a central generation model where everybody gets the same power at the same rate, within a given customer class.

Tucker: While we're really talking about all clean forms of energy-powering microgrids, today I want to talk a little bit more about propane-fueled microgrids. And I know you're working on two: you mentioned one in San Diego, and then one is, I guess, in development north of you in Minnesota. Can you talk to us about those projects where propane is playing a role, and maybe how that all fits together?

Michael: The San Pasqual Band in Southern California and San Diego County, we're working on a microgrid with them that's going to be using primarily photovoltaic solar, combining that in a system that has lithium ferro-phosphate batteries, and then it's using propane as essentially a standby generation source. If there's a long-duration power outage caused by one of the public safety power shutoffs that they have been experiencing in that part of the state, and if it's over a few days or a couple of days, the batteries are going to get drained. In order to keep their vital systems going at their tribal administration campus, there's propane available to provide power at night and to recharge those batteries, if need be, so that they can continue to operate their tribal law enforcement, their tribal hall. And it's got a Red Cross evacuation center, as well as an education building, their fire department. Those kinds of things are all on the same campus there. So, it's a great project, really important for that community.

It's a great example of a microgrid project that offers not only resilience but also equity to an underserved part of the country. San Diego County is a hot, dry climate and has its own unique power needs. I asked about the microgrid project in Minnesota, a part of the country with a different climate profile.

Michael: Way up by the Canadian border at the Red Lake Wildlife Management Area, the Minnesota Department of Natural Resources has its headquarters for a very large region of far northern Minnesota in a heavy wilderness area. And they are at the end of a long old power line that was really never intended to be operating as long as it has been, and there are practically no customers in between. And the co-op that serves them has said, "Every time this thing has a problem, it's costing us more to fix it than you pay us in a year for power bills, and so next time it goes down, it's on you to repair it."

The answer was to cut the cord to their co-op and build an off-grid system. In fact, there are two systems, because the headquarters itself is at Norris Camp, and the manager's residence is about a mile away.

Michael: It's powering the home there as well as a garage, with solar power located on a ground-mounted array in a clearing out in the forest, right up against an old-growth woods, so it was pretty complicated from a sighting perspective to figure out how that's going to work. But we made it work, and propane is indispensable to make that a reliable system. It gets extremely cold up there. We were, in fact, in the middle of the design last winter when the temperature dropped to around forty degrees below zero. They use propane for heating and for cooking and things. Their experience has been that, even when it does get that cold, there's enough energy, heat inertia in the system that it continues to vaporize. They didn't want to use diesel out in the middle of the north woods; it's so pristine up there. And nevertheless, it works in far northern Minnesota, and it works in far southern California and everywhere in between.

Tucker: What do these systems have to offer in terms of grid independence and resiliency for at-risk communities in general?

Michael: Public safety power shutoffs are being driven by the fact that the central power transmission system isn't safe. What we're seeing already is a movement by communities to try and shore up their power, because they cannot deal with these many days of power outages happening every single fire season. The utilities are mobilizing there. The California Public Utilities Commission and the Energy Commission are working with utilities to try and help them to adapt and to support microgrids, frankly, and also other solutions that reduce those kinds of risks.[1]

Jeffrey Schlegelmilch, the disaster preparedness expert, had some thoughts about microgrids as well. His take focused on equity.

Jeffrey: By putting microgrids in socially vulnerable neighborhoods, they're able to keep the lights on during disasters. In turn, not only does this help the most at-risk people, but it also helps the surrounding areas by keeping businesses running and mitigating the overall risks to the community. We're going to see microgrids in some vulnerable areas to show that it was done and to demonstrate the technology, but, ultimately, it'll be an imbalance where wealthier areas are going to benefit from microgrids because they have more capacity to advocate for those kinds of investments.

He said these inequities can be addressed with targeted investment as we move down the path to zero.

Jeffrey: We'll see it as an opportunity. We looked at the new data coming out and the information we have on the inequities of disaster and the potential for outsized benefit from investing in areas that can benefit the most. And we see this really as a great equalizer in what'll probably be some of the greatest investments in the grid that we've seen in the last century.

Tucker: I want to switch it up on you a bit. I read in the *Washington Post* today that the idea that we can keep emitting greenhouse gases and later buy our way out of it with adaptation just doesn't make any sense. Now, you're a person who's really studied this concept of cause and effect and preparation and response. How do you respond to this critique of adaptation?

Jeffrey: There are no simple answers when it comes to disasters. We're not going to meet the global emissions reduction targets that have been set by the UN, by the Paris Agreements, by the various internationals, but we need to keep pursuing it.[2] We need to keep reducing greenhouse gas emissions. We absolutely need to. It's the root cause of a lot of the disasters we're facing. The reality is that we need to spend a lot more on adaptation, because we are already experiencing the consequences of it, and we're going to continue to experience increasing consequences of it. Even when we look at renewables: Is it solar? Is it wind? Is it carbon capture to help offset transitional fuels, like you mentioned? New clean propane? Things like that. It really has to be all of the above. When we're talking about microgrids, ultimately the benefit is that it gives options. And that's how we manage uncertainty going into the future: we give ourselves as many options as possible.

MAGIC WANDS

I asked Jeffrey Schlegelmilch and Michael Burr what one thing they would do with the *Path to Zero* magic wand that would have the biggest climate impact.

83

Jeffrey: I think to avert these increases, we take all the carbon out of the atmosphere, but that doesn't actually fix the problem. It just kicks it down the road, because we're still emitting it. We have to change economies, whole economies and whole value streams that are based on that. But then we still have disasters from policies that have led to wide disparities in terms of access to the benefits of civil society. What we really need to do is look at the range of behaviors that people are likely to take, steer them toward the one that's most beneficial, and write our plans around that rather than try to force people to do what our plan says they should do. That's a really important insight into acknowledging that there are trends in human behavior that we're trying too hard to predict and control, rather than build systems that accommodate fundamentally who we are.

Michael: What I would like to do is eliminate climate change denialism. And that comes down to this: can we please get past being so focused on our own personal self-interests that we're incapable of looking at the facts and accepting them as reality, so that we can try to improve the situation? The data is clear; the data is very well established. The climate has already changed. It has changed. Climate change isn't something that's coming. It's already happened. It's happening. And if we don't, as a people, get our arms around that and face that, it's going to be that much more difficult to try and slow it down, try to correct the problem, and to adapt to it.

I share the concerns of these two futurists. While we adapt to climate change by using a 3-D grid philosophy, we cannot lose our focus on decarbonization. The reliability improvements we make can have immediate impact on people's lives and livelihoods in the disasters we're seeing, but oversimplification gets us into more trouble. Decarbonizing the grid is critical. We have to find a way to do it without putting a massive financial burden on the shoulders of the most vulnerable in the process.

WIDENING THE PATH

If you're interested in the 3-D grid or the adaptations that can help us get to a net zero future, consider these ideas:

- In Season 5 of *Path to Zero*, I had a great conversation with Dr. Bruce Usher of Columbia University about climate change finance.[3] Learn more by reading his book, *Investing in the Era of Climate Change*, an expert guide to the risks and opportunities for investors as the world faces climate change. He details how to finance the winners and avoid the losers in a transforming global economy.

- Can you install a microgrid for your business or perhaps a small neighborhood? It's interesting to think about energy security as your reason to invest in adaptation and resilience. If you live in a weather-vulnerable region, you may want to consider making an individual microgrid investment.

- Change your computer passwords. Yes, cyber criminals are attacking the grid every day, but they're doing the same thing to your bank accounts, credit cards, and more to try to steal personal information that can lead them to your utility bill. We often don't think of ourselves as a failure point for grid security, but like Colonial Pipeline discovered, it takes only one poorly designed password to crack open a big piece of today's grid. Until we're fully 3-D, we're vulnerable to ever more sophisticated disruptions.

CHAPTER 4

Diesel's Last Decade

We cannot solve our problems with the same thinking
we used when we created them.

—Albert Einstein

An entrepreneur coach named Dan Sullivan encourages his clients to ask a question that goes like this: "It's three years from today, and you are looking back with great satisfaction. What has happened for you to feel this way?" I've got an answer: diesel engines are no longer made. It may take longer than three years, so let's call it 2030. At the beginning of that decade, we'll be able to look back and declare the 2020s as diesel's last decade.

As we walk the path to zero, we should replace more bad things while adding more good things, and diesel tops my list of the former. Rudolf Diesel, the German engineer who invented the eponymous engine in 1893, first used peanut oil to power his invention.[1] He eventually turned to the crude oil–derived diesel fuel we know today, and while it has been crucial to the development of modern society, it's time to say goodbye to this highly carbon-intensive energy. We do well to remember that Mr. Diesel was an inventor, and inventors are driven to create new and better things for the world, so my bet is that he would agree.

About 85 percent of diesel fuel's mass is carbon, and when burned, a great deal of carbon is released into the atmosphere. The CO2 emission from diesel is actually slightly lower than from gasoline (73.25 g/MJ vs. 73.38 g/MJ) and isn't nearly as bad as kerosene or coal, but it's still high.[2]

The World Health Organization has labeled diesel emissions carcinogenic. The reason? Exhaust from diesel engines is full of criteria pollutants—on the order of six to ten times higher than from gasoline engines.[3] Of the six criteria pollutants defined by the Clean Air Act, diesel exhaust bellows out four:

- Carbon monoxide (CO) – Exposure to elevated CO may result in reduced oxygen to the heart.

- Nitrogen dioxide (NO_2) – Diesel engines are responsible for 85 percent of all NO_2 emissions from mobile sources, and NO_2 is a big contributor to smog.

- Sulfur dioxide (SO_2) – SO_2 is another big smog contributor and an acid-rain accelerant.

- Particulate matter (PM) – The black soot you see coming out of the exhaust pipe contains microscopic solids or liquid droplets so small they can be inhaled, resulting in negative impacts to your heart and lungs.

Smog, acid rain, soil and water pollution, heart and lung disease, respiratory damage, and even premature death are all connected to criteria pollutant exposure—and not just in the United States. The European Environment Agency found that nitrogen dioxide (NO2) from diesel fumes had caused around 71,000 premature deaths across the continent in a single year.[4]

Diesel's last decade is already in motion. Two years ago, Volvo pledged it would never again launch a new car with a diesel engine.[5] BMW is ending production of two of its popular diesel engines, and the California Air Resources Board (CARB) is requiring truck manufacturers to begin the transition from diesel to zero-emission trucks in 2024.[6] CARB says trucks are to blame for 70 percent of the smog-causing pollution and 80 percent of carcinogenic diesel soot in the state.

You might think all this talk about eliminating diesel engines also means the end of internal combustion engines. As legendary football coach Lee Corso famously says, "not so fast, my friends."[7]

The opposite is true, in fact. The internal combustion engine (ICE) is better than ever and getting better every day.

TIME JUMP TO 2050

Once again, we have arrived in our 2050 future, and transportation looks a lot different than it did back in the 2020s, diesel's last decade. As diesel died, we converted most of the school buses in America to renewable propane. Not only did this help achieve our net zero reality, but the savings in fuel and maintenance costs alone was enough to hire 23,000 new schoolteachers for students across the country.

Propane-powered school buses equipped with newer engines also emit 94 percent fewer NOx emissions and six percent fewer life cycle CO_2 emissions. Unlike diesel, propane buses do not require costly after-treatment systems and exhaust fluid to mitigate emissions. Particulate matter emissions from propane school buses on a typical operation cycle are near zero.

We learned from experience that the electrification of heavy-duty vehicles was the wrong solution. In the 2020s, electric transit bus costs were as much as $400,000, versus $100,000 for a propane-powered bus, and a 350-kW single port DC fast charger came with a price tag of $140,000.[8] We also came to realize that buses and large trucks require two 8,000-pound lithium-ion batteries, which exceeded strict federal weight limits and, therefore, decreased payload capacity.[9]

Remarkably, the internal combustion engine made it to this future with us. In the 2020s, the entire European Union was set to ban ICEs, and then, as reported, "Germany changed its mind." What happened?[10]

In that particular case, the Germans argued that new synthetic fuels (many of which we talked about in the previous chapter) were an answer to carbon emissions. As right as they were about that idea, two guests on *Path to Zero* in 2022 made the bigger difference to me.

Felix Leach and Kelly Senecal

June 3, 2022 • Season 3 • Episode 10

TWO EXPERTS on automotive engineering, Dr. Felix Leach, an associate professor of engineering at the University of Oxford, and Dr. Kelly Senecal, cofounder and owner of Convergent Science, a computational fluid dynamic software company, coauthored the book *Racing Toward Zero: The Untold Story of Driving Green*. Their book changed my view of the lifespan of ICEs. They started our conversation with a straightforward premise: Most vehicles on the planet use the internal combustion engine, so improving its technology from the engine design all the way to the fuels it uses can have a huge immediate impact on reducing emissions globally.

Since Felix lives in Oxford, England, and Kelly lives in Madison, Wisconsin, I was curious how these two leaders met and ended up writing a book together.

Dr. Senecal: 2017 is the year I like to call "[the year] combustion died." Of course, I'm saying that sarcastically, but that's really when a lot of press came out about the combustion engine being dead. I really started to pick up some advocacy in that area, saying "Hey, wait a minute, don't forget about the internal combustion engine. And around that time, Felix had written, along with some other UK academics, a response to an article from the *Economist* called, "The Death of the Internal Combustion Engine."[1] And he was making a lot of the same points that I was making as well. And so, I was like, "Who is this guy?" And I tracked him down at a conference we both attended in Capri, Italy. And we just hit it off from there and have been working together ever since. Felix, if you want to add something to the story there...

Dr. Leach: No, I think the only thing I would add is that I think Kelly and I independently had been unaware that we were doing the same stuff. There was a lot of loss of trust in the auto industry generally. And this was manifesting itself as, yeah, the death of the internal combustion engine. And I thought that this would be really damaging. And so, I ring-led a letter back to the *Economist* after this article they wrote, saying, "Actually, we don't think you're right, and here's why." And to their credit, they published it. And that's the genesis of our meeting. And Kelly and I haven't looked back really yet, one book and several academic papers later.

Tucker: Felix, what is your area of research at Oxford?

Dr. Leach: My background is very much in emissions, from internal combustion engines, particularly with different fuels. My PhD was on the effect of fuel competition on particulates. But I've expanded more broadly than that. So today, I investigate new fuels, both ones that contain carbon and ones that don't contain carbon, such as ammonia and hydrogen, but also looking at hybrid powertrains and particularly what combustion engines might be best for ultra-high efficiency hybrid powertrains. So, I've got quite a diverse set of interest these days, but all around propulsion and energy.

Tucker: I've studied the European position when it comes to the future of greener vehicles myself, which I see as slightly different from the American position in broader terms of how we're going to address climate. Europe shifted from being almost completely focused on diesel, then literally overnight said, "diesel is bad," then pivoted straight to coal-powered battery electric, even though, now, it is quite obvious that your electric grid is probably even more starved for electrons than the US grid. So, how are fleet managers in Europe reacting to the about-face away from diesel?

Dr. Leach: Tucker, it's such a good question. I mean, I think a fleet manager follows the incentives that they're given. And the thing about fleets is that they tend to get renewed fairly quickly, say in two or three years, typically, a fleet would rotate. The problem is, of course: what are the consequences of that? Most fleets aren't driven into the ground; they're sold on the second-hand market, and you end up with a market of vehicles that's very eclectic. And I think what people have been saying is that this one-size-fits-all strategy hasn't worked for Europe in the past. Diesel was good in some respects, but bad in others, and everyone was saying, "Well, just be careful with what you're doing here." And they went, like you say, straight down the diesel pathway.

Tucker: Are you suggesting that today's approach to battery electric vehicles is the same?

Dr. Leach: I think more and more people are beginning to cotton onto battery electric vehicles. They're brilliant in many ways, but they're not the solution to everything. And so, by pursuing this one-size-fits-all strategy again and again in Europe, we keep making mistakes, and history keeps repeating itself roughly once a decade.

Tucker: I have one more question for you. I'm often struck by how the US and Europe seem to have almost a singular obsession around climate and GHG and CO_2 and temperature rise, when in fact, to me the near-term and more silent killer, if you will, could easily be bronchitis, asthma, COPD that's created by poor lung health, poor plant health that comes to us directly as a result of particulate matter and NOx. As a person who studies that, how do you find a balance between focus on climate and focus on health?

Dr. Leach: What a million-dollar question. I think "pollution" is not a helpful word. I think we often mislead people when we start talking about pollution from vehicles, because it's exactly as you say, do you mean CO_2 or greenhouse gas emissions? Is that pollution? Or are you talking about NOx and particulate matter and all these other emissions that come out of vehicles? We want to reduce them all. Of course we do. But it's a balance, like you say, between perhaps something that's going to kill you or me with bronchitis or whatever or something that might kill our grandchildren, great-grandchildren, great-great-grandchildren, and so on in the future.

We have the technical solutions today to deal with the non-CO_2 emissions from vehicles. The technology today is brilliant. Sometimes we lose sight of that by considering vehicles from the '50s, '60s that had clouds of black smoke coming out of them, that you could smell before you saw them on the freeway. Today, that's not the reality.

Tucker: Yeah, thank you. So, Kelly, let's turn to you for a moment. I think you would be considered, by any measure, a world-class expert in computational fluid dynamics. To the uninitiated, we often shorten that to CFD, the modern term in engineering. And I know you've really been around one of the great mechanical engineering universities in the world, University of Wisconsin at Madison. But talk to us about your work at Convergent Science and, really, how you got to this point to write the book and be so invested in improving the internal combustion engine.

Dr. Senecal: Essentially, we're modeling things like engines or things like flow over airplanes, aerodynamics, on the computer. So, instead of doing the experiments, we simulate the device on the computer, and hopefully we can improve it, make design decisions in a cheaper way, before we cut metal and before we actually design it. Being on the inside and really knowing how engines work and a lot of the technology that Felix alluded to about controlling the criteria pollutants and all of this, they're not nearly as bad as we're making them out to be. So that's what pushed me down this advocacy route into the book. It just felt like there was a real need to put this out there.

Tucker: So let me ask both of you. Do you believe that the internal combustion engine is dead?

Dr. Senecal: Well, should it be dead? No. For sure, it should not be dead. We like to say, "It's not the engine that's the problem;

it's the fuel." And so, there's a long runway there for the engine. There are a lot of applications where, even if we think we want to electrify everything, we won't be able to. And then there's the question of, is it dead in terms of policy? Do I think diesel bans are really going to happen? I think they'll try in some countries, but I think they're going to realize it doesn't make any sense. So, short answer is no, I don't think the internal combustion engine is dead.

Dr. Leach: No. Simple answer. I think I'd perhaps covered it from a slightly different perspective than Kelly, not least because Europe has taken quite a different path to the US at the moment. In some respects, we're further along the path toward bans. But, as you said yourself, Tucker, internal combustion engines could be in anything from a chainsaw to an oil tanker ship. So, we just need to think about what the application is. Will they be in everything that they are today in the future? No, of course they won't.

But the challenge here is not necessarily the internal combustion engine; it's the fuel we use to power it, right? I think that we can get toward renewable fuels. And, whether that's hydrogen or something else, e-fuels made from electricity and renewable energy, then why would we need to kill the internal combustion engine? Because it too can be part of our sustainable future.

Tucker: I know you address it some in your book, but one of the things that I never hear politicians talk about or even anyone really engaging in the debate truly talk about is the cost of running alternatives to internal combustion engines. The presumption always is that because electricity could be cheaper, that the cost to operate a battery electric vehicle will be cheaper. I always think about cost from the fleet manager's perspective—cost per mile, cost per drop, however you want to think about it. Do you see that battery electric will have an economic advantage in cost per mile over time, over an IC engine?

Dr. Leach: I hate conversations about cost, because I'm not an economist, but what I do see from a European perspective is that cost is a really tricky area to answer because there are so many subsidies, both hidden and less hidden, both for internal combustion engines and for battery electric vehicles. But, at the moment, our electricity prices are going up, not down, in part because of global shifts toward different types of production. I struggle to see how that will make things cheaper.

Tucker: I, too, am not an economist, but I will say with total certainty, the cost of electricity will rise across the continent and the world, because of a variety of issues. But while the sun may be free and the wind may blow free, to harness that power to put it in places where people want to use it is a challenge.

Dr. Leach: It's not just about where you generate electricity; it's also about when you generate it, and then, importantly, storing it. One of the nice things about gasoline and diesel is that they are energy stores. And you store enough energy to drive, what? 4,500 miles in a 50-, a 100-liter fuel tank on a vehicle. To do that with raw electricity in batteries, you need much, much larger volume and, indeed, weight. So, I think energy storage on a grid scale will also be really important. Certainly, there are days when, in the UK in particular, the wind isn't blowing and the sun's not shining in the winter. This alone poses a problem for the reliability of wind- and solar-generated electricity in EVs if we were to take away diesel and gasoline-powered vehicles altogether.

Tucker: Right. Energy storage on a grid scale is certainly not even in its infancy today, the way we store it in batteries. As we think about the future of transportation, how has the narrative become that the only path forward is this narrow path toward electrification?

Dr. Senecal: If you call something a "zero-emission vehicle," people are going to believe such a thing exists. But the real problem is we regulate them that way. We regulate the tailpipe, which made sense in the 1970s, when pretty much every vehicle on the road had a tailpipe. And that's where most of the emissions come from on an internal combustion engine vehicle. They come from other places, as well, but most of it comes from the tailpipe.

We've essentially moved the tailpipe away from the vehicle in a lot of cases, but yet we still regulate the tailpipe. That is a major problem. Auto companies actually like that, because now when they do their fleet averaging on their CO_2 emissions, for example, they can take a big zero for that electric vehicle, sometimes even more than one zero, if that makes sense. Anything multiplied by zero is still zero, but they can count it as, say, two cars or one and a half cars or whatever. That allows them to sell their big trucks, right?

As soon as we start to look at the whole life cycle analysis about where all the emissions are formed, you start to realize that, certainly, electric vehicles can be very clean. But in other parts of the world, it makes more sense to drive a hybrid, based on the electricity grid.

Tucker: In my experience working with fleets or automakers, I've observed a reluctance to use hybrids in favor of either straight internal combustion or straight battery electric. Why do you think there has not been a revolution toward hybrids?

Dr. Leach: We live in a world where battery electric vehicles have some efforts toward decarbonization, but there aren't enough of them, and there are not going to be enough of them rapidly. If the only acceptable answer out of a tailpipe is zero, a hybrid's not going to be zero in that sense. But . . . if you've moved the emissions to the power plant, it still counts as zero. I think hybrids are struggling because of the legislative and regulatory framework that they're placed in. That doesn't mean they're not brilliant technology. A better option would be to make every vehicle a hybrid by 2025. That's a much more achievable goal, and you'd get faster decarbonization.

Tucker: There are already examples of hybrids on the market today that are hugely popular, are lowering emissions while saving their drivers money, and many—if not most—vehicle owners may not even realize they are driving a hybrid.

Dr. Senecal: So, the new version of the Toyota Sienna only comes out as a full hybrid. They went from a vehicle that was, say, mid-20s mpg to something that's like mid-30s mpg by making it a full hybrid. People are buying it like hotcakes. And they're getting much better fuel economy, and obviously that means less CO_2.

Tucker: The real benefit of a hybrid, whether it's a partial or full hybrid, is that it's allowing the two portions, the internal combustion portion, or the hybrid portion, to be as effective as they can possibly be together. It makes each engine able to be more optimized, and that's really how you move from 20 mpg to 30 mpg.

Dr. Leach: You are enabling both parts of the powertrain so that the engine and the electric motors and batteries operate at their most efficient points, but you also get to recover energy at the same time. So, for example, when you brake in a non-hybridized vehicle, that energy is just wasted as heat through your brake pads, whereas, in a hybrid vehicle, you can use that to stick that energy right back in the battery and use it again.

Tucker: A decade ago, hybrid technology was somewhat unproven and expensive and heavy, and the systems that talk to each other were a bit cumbersome. As we look forward, those systems are both reliable and lighter and more cost-effective. Hybrid systems today and in the future have tremendous advantage for power efficiency, for emissions, and for cost over even an electric battery vehicle in many applications. Would you agree?

Dr. Senecal: For sure. I like to say that there should be a small battery in every vehicle, whether that's a hybrid or a full battery electric. We're being smart about how we use battery resources, which we're seeing today as a real issue. The excuse out there from a lot of folks is that with two different powertrains, we have two things that can go wrong and it's the worst of both worlds. I like to say it's the best of both worlds. I think hybrids are the fastest way we can reduce CO_2 today.

In their book, *Racing Toward Zero*, Felix and Kelly assert that engines aren't where the most gains can be made when it comes to carbon emissions; the fuel is. So, I asked what they thought the future of hydrogen is in transportation.

Dr. Leach: I think this is a great question, and I think the honest answer is we don't yet know. There's going to be a huge demand for hydrogen that we'll struggle to fill, but I think it'll probably start at the heaviest end of transportation. In a world where people perceive that batteries will decarbonize everything, there is a limit to how much a battery electric vehicle can do in terms of the very heavy end of the market. So, I'm talking about maybe Class 8 trucks and larger, very heavy off-road machinery, because the amount of energy you need to store in batteries results in the batteries just weighing too much. I think it will be used in other areas as well, such as home heating.

Dr. Senecal: Let's not forget that hydrogen is far from zero emissions as well. Most of the hydrogen we make today, it isn't green hydrogen made from renewable electricity. But technology is constantly evolving, and this is the reason why we need to not ban technologies. Because as soon as you put a ban on the internal combustion engine, you're basically telling the world, "This isn't going to be around." We need students to be the next generation of engineers and scientists working to improve these things. If they're not going into the area, then we can't improve the technology. Things like hydrogen, internal combustion engines, low carbon, zero carbon fuels, they have big potential, and so that's why I think we need to be very careful about banning things.

Tucker: I couldn't agree more. Felix, do you see a future for engines using biodiesel and renewable propane, perhaps?

Dr. Leach: I certainly do. I think the challenge with all renewables is getting enough of them. The amount of energy we currently take from fossil fuels is vast, and that's why I love your silver buckshot analogy. I think we're going to need all of these things. I think renewable fuels, whether it's DME, biodiesel, or whatever you want to throw at it, we're going to need all of these things. And so, I'm a huge proponent for them, because we've got such a huge task to replace all of this fossil-derived energy, and I think biofuels, e-fuels, all of these things will be really important.

Tucker: As we begin to replace large power plants, natural gas fire, diesel fire, coal fire with solar wind, I keep waiting for the mathematicians to realize that those large power plants produce a lot more power than these distributed, smaller solar wind farms and that we're going to be short on electricity without these energy-dense, lower-carbon fuels, like propane or natural gas, and even nuclear. You'll never have the systems you need for combustion, for transportation, for heating your homes when it's cold.

Dr. Leach: I think there is an acknowledgment that nuclear will be a big part of that, because you get a lot of power out of a relatively small footprint in the same way that you do with a gas power station, for example.

Tucker: In the work we've done with Cummins, we were able to reduce CO2 emissions from the engine and the fuel and meet the thermal efficiency of diesel, cutting CO2 emissions. I am convinced by these early results that internal combustion engines can be perfected to generate more power and fewer emissions.

Dr. Senecal: There is a perception that we've reached the pinnacle with the IC engine, and there's nowhere to go, and there certainly is a place to go. There's certainly room to improve engines, and we see it every day. Not only with computational fluid dynamics, but there's a lot of really great experimental work out there.

One example I like to talk about is the Skyactive X engine from Mazda. With this engine, Mazda was able to employ an advanced combustion recipe, which they call "SPCCI." This was a spinoff of HCCI, Homogeneous Charge Compression Ignition, which has been the holy grail that people had been chasing for a long time in the combustion space. However, HCCI came with challenges; namely, it had trouble working across the operating map. Mazda was able to avoid some of these issues and make SPCCI work practically and efficiently.

Incremental changes . . . really add up in the end. There's definitely more room to improve the internal combustion engine. Not just the fuel but the engine itself.

Tucker: Felix, what final thought would you leave with our listeners?

Dr. Leach: If anyone comes up and says, "It's really simple. I've got a solution to solve the challenging issue of transportation's carbon problems," it's a really complex set of intertwined things, and the more I look at it, the more I realize how challenging and complex it is . . . anyone who comes up and says, "I've got a solution. It's going to be really easy"—they're putting you on. Don't believe them.

MAGIC WANDS

Cicero himself said, "Brevity is the best recommendation of speech, whether in a senator or an orator." If he is right, then both Felix and Kelly qualify for the Senate! In asking them to wave their magic wands to give us one thing they would like to see happen that would have the biggest climate impact, both were brief and, at the same time, bold.

Dr. Leach: I would create energy storage technology on a grid scale that would work.

Dr. Senecal: I'll keep it on transportation, and I'll say . . . changing the regulations. Making the regulations based on the entire life cycle and not just the tailpipe. That's what I would do. I think that would have the biggest impact on transportation, CO2.

WIDENING THE PATH

We need help from our policymakers to understand that engines and fuels must be part of a wide-path solution to a net zero future.

- Very few policymakers have a background in science. In a world of professional politicians, it's not that legislatures don't want to make policies that impact the climate for the better; they simply don't have the knowledge to do so. This is why it takes experts like Kelly and Felix, people like you and me, to educate those around us.

- Toyota's philosophy is worth studying, especially in the area of IC-hybrid engines. It is making remarkable advances every day on the path to zero emissions.[2]

- "Well-to-Wheel" is a method to evaluate the efficiency and emissions of an energy source by considering its entire life cycle, and we should adopt it as a standard measurement. The well-to-wheel method provides the most complete and accurate way to measure energy consumption and greenhouse gas emissions. We will live in a future where tailpipes disappear, but carbon emissions don't. The reason is that tailpipe emission measures will give way to a full carbon lifecycle analysis, known as Scope 3 impacts.[3] For us to get better, we have to be better at measuring and accepting a view from behind the plug and before the tailpipe.

CHAPTER 5

Energy, Economy, Environment

*Economic growth and environmental protection
are not at odds. They're opposite sides of the same coin
if you're looking at longer-term prosperity.*
—HENRY PAULSON

T he Arhuacos are an indigenous tribe in Colombia. They grow everything they need—coffee, beans, bananas, and sugar cane—using ancient farming practices and manual labor.[1] Families cook meals over open fires inside rudimentary, poorly ventilated huts where temperatures reach 120 degrees F. While the fire makes food preparation possible, it also produces smoke that fills the lungs, which is a significant reason why only half of the Arhuaco children ever make it to adulthood.[2]

Dr. Scott Tinker, director of the Bureau of Economic Geology at the University of Texas, who is also the state

111

geologist of Texas and a documentary filmmaker, is one of the most influential geologists in the world. In his 2020 documentary, *Switch On*, he puts a spotlight on the Arhuacos and says, "There are another 1 billion people, most of them urban, with limited energy that's often unaffordable or dangerous.[3] Nearly all of these people, and a few hundred million more, still burn wood, straw, dung, and other biomass for cooking or heating and suffer from breathing its smoke."

Along with all of his other titles, Scott is the founder and chairman of Switch Energy Alliance, a non-partisan 501(c)(3) that seeks to educate people about energy through inspirational film. This chapter summarizes my fascinating conversation with Scott, what I learned from him about the triad of energy, the economy, and the environment, and how these must be aligned in order for real change, and our net zero future, to happen.

Scott Tinker

May 24, 2021 • Season 2 • Episode 12

THE ARHUACOS—and the nearly one billion other people like them living without electricity—survive in what the United Nations calls "energy poverty." The UN estimates that "about 2.6 billion, a third of the world's population, have no access to clean cooking fuels."[1] When I interviewed him for my *Path to Zero* podcast in 2021, Scott told me he has seen this up close.[2]

Dr. Tinker: I saw the absolute poorest of the poor and the richest of the rich. People are trying to improve themselves in life. All of us are. You want your kids to have a better life than you had. That's just a common theme, globally.

In order to do that, Scott told me, those living in energy poverty must figure out a way to evolve from survivability to stability. Without sufficient energy, people experiencing energy poverty can't imagine upward economic mobility, and we cannot expect them to be participants in decarbonization. The fuels that make the energy they use to survive—indoor wood-burning fires and other biomass, for example—contribute to global warming. It may not be good for the environment or their health, but they need the cheapest possible fuels available simply to live.

The path to net zero emissions is not going to be symmetrical. For some countries, the journey will be faster. For other parts of the world, like these remote, tribal areas, the journey will be different. This is why the path has to be wide, flexible, and bespoke to the needs of people. It does little good for the Arhuacos' homes to be electrified, for example, when they don't have electric appliances.

Roger Pielke Jr., author of *The Honest Broker: Making Sense of Science in Policy and Politics*, makes this point crystal clear when he says, "If there is an iron law of climate policy, it is that when policies focused on economic growth confront policies focused on emissions reductions, it is economic growth that will win out every time."[3]

On the path to zero, we will encounter problems that are very difficult to leap over. In those cases, incremental improvements are just as important and powerful. Solutions we can implement today, working within the constraints of the iron law, can and should be high on our priority list.

TIME JUMP TO 2050

Here in 2050, net zero is a reality in the United States. America is an example to the rest of the world; however, net zero is not a uniform proposition around the world. Developing countries with extreme poverty, "run by autocrats . . . not particularly keen on getting [clean energy] to their people," are extraordinary barriers to progress," Scott Tinker warned me back in 2021. He reminded me that once people are educated, they begin to have opinions and want a say in how they are governed. Even here in the 2050s, those are dangerous ideas to dictators.

The history books of 2050, however, record how people, like members of the 1860s Granger movement in America, pushed past obstructions to create community energy systems and self-governed cooperatives.[4] Clean energy co-ops formed when people were introduced to the health benefits of alternative energy sources. This led to economic growth, which, in turn, opened the way for people to serve as better stewards of the environment.

Luckily, we also had enough experience to know that preserving cultural identity was as important as modernizing living standards. Back in the 2020s, Bob Freling, executive director of the non-profit Solar Electric Light Fund (SELF), told Scott when he interviewed him for *Switch On*, "We would never go and impose our solutions on a community that has not invited us. We are very mindful that not everybody in the world wants this." SELF acknowledged that "solutions to energy poverty were not one-size-fits-all. Different communities had different priorities. Energy projects had to consider these priorities in establishing objectives and determining the best models to meet them."

Cooking for Life™, a campaign of the World Liquid Propane Gas Association, was another example.[5] It worked to "facilitate the transition of one billion people from cooking with traditional fuels, as well as other dirty and dangerous fuels, such as kerosene, to cleaner-burning LPG." The organization gave policy makers in the emerging world the tools and resources necessary to bring energy conversion programs to their people, and, on a practical level, to replace the burning of straw, dung, wood, and plants with clean-burning propane. Their goal was to meet this transition by the year 2030, and in 2050, the organization has surpassed its goals. It has helped to relieve energy poverty around the world by equipping remote villages and tribes with propane and propane stoves.

Cooking for Life and other likeminded organizations solved the problem of dirty fuels, but in doing so they created another challenge—dependency on imported fuels, posing a challenge to energy independence or energy security.

Like every challenge on the path to zero, this problem had to be solved next. Pielke's "iron law" and the energy-economy-environment sequence Tinker talked about played out just as it had many times before:

1. Those in energy poverty were supplied with cleaner energy.

2. They stayed alive and began to thrive.

3. Investments in new technologies created energy independence and sustainability at the same time.

Scott brought me back to the present day to explain his view of the energy transition. He talked about how his view has been shaped after traveling to more than sixty-five countries. Today, Scott believes it's his duty, and the duty of the developed world, to lift people from poverty to prosperity.

Dr. Tinker: That's the real transition. The energy transition to me is not from one fuel to another. It's from poverty to prosperity. When that happens, we will have succeeded in many ways. Just purely from human rights . . . that to me is the most important mission on Earth. The worst environments in the world are where it's poor, without exception. They just can't afford it. That's why the order is important: energy, economy, environment. Energy, economy, environment.

We don't have to look far to see what happens when people go without electricity for a few days. When Winter Storm Uri hit Texas in February 2021, more than 240 people died in the massive power outage that lasted for days.[6]

Dr. Tinker: Two thirds of the world live that way all the time, without much or any electricity. They don't have any, or it's very unreliable. They live like [Texans] lived for a week in February all the time.

In contrast to China and India, who together account for two thirds of the world's population, there are about 570 million people in North America and Western Europe combined—just over 7 percent of the world's population.[7]

Dr. Tinker: The other 93 percent are just emerging and industrializing and growing and developing their economies. The cleanest air in the world is in the US, and we have one of the largest economies because we can afford to clean it up. This is the link between energy, the economy, and the environment. Energy underpins economies. Economies invest in the environment. That little dance drives everything. If you try to skip some points, it just doesn't work. You get that energy; you start to grow and industrialize. Your education goes up. Directly tied to that is lower birth rates. Population growth slows, which is positive.

He explained that lower birth rates and the slow-down in population growth result in more rights and greater freedom, particularly for women.

Dr. Tinker: They're going for the water and cooking indoors with wood and biomass and dying literally by the millions of various lung cancers.[8] They're disproportionately disadvantaged by energy poverty.

Tucker: Some suggest world economies grow to the detriment of the environment, but you flip this idea on its head a little bit: that a focus on people will ultimately help the planet.

Dr. Tinker: I'm talking about a modern economy. Sure, we could have a very clean environment without humans. Maybe some people would prefer that. I've actually had people tell me that. Let's just pretend like there are no humans. There are 7.8 billion of us and growing. Most want to grow and develop. We've got to unpin the bottom end, the plus or minus billion people living in extreme poverty without much energy at all, then another couple billion in emerging economies that are starting to develop.

Scott and his colleagues are seeking some practical solutions for how energy, economics, and the environment can all work together for a cleaner, more sustainable future. On a regular basis, he takes on three questions:

1. "What would have to happen to achieve net zero?"
2. "Should it happen?"
3. "Can it happen?"

In addressing the first question, he referenced a 2021 report from the IEA (International Energy Agency) about what would need to happen in order to achieve net zero emissions by 2050.[9] The report outlines an ambitious goal of expanding solar capacity.

Dr. Tinker: Should it happen, and can it happen? Those are harder questions. When you're talking about having to build the world's largest solar park every day until 2030 to get there, well, that's not going to happen.[10] You can't build the world's largest solar park every single day for the next thirty years. It's hard to understand the scale of energy consumption and demand. Most people don't know where electricity comes from, but the challenge is they think they do.

Tucker: A lot of people see solar and wind power as silver-bullet solutions. I would argue that they're part of the solution, but they're limited.

Dr. Tinker: The sun isn't the same everywhere; neither is the wind. They're resources. Even if you're in the better, windier places and in the sunnier places, you still have to collect it.

The collection systems pose yet another tax on the energy-economy-environment triad. Building the solar panels and wind turbines takes a lot of energy. Since these natural, renewable resources aren't always available—if the sun isn't shining or the wind isn't blowing—they must employ either backup plants (burning) or batteries, which are heavily dependent on mining for minerals.

Dr. Tinker: Whenever I ask students if they think mining and manufacturing and landfill disposal are green, they shake their head and say, "Of course not." I say, "Well, why are solar and wind and batteries considered green?" We connect the three dots. It's a moment. It's always a moment where they think, "Wow." The climate is a big piece of the environment, but so are the land and the air and the water. Those are the pillars of the environment. You can't disadvantage the land and the air and the water in order to address one. Anytime you go too far in the direction of something, you hurt the others. This is the challenge. It's thinking a little bit more critically than just black and white, good and bad, clean and dirty, believer, denier. It is not binary. It's more complex than that.

It's an idea he tries to convey through Switch Energy Alliance. Through Switch, he emphasizes taking a sensible approach to energy's future. The Alliance is focusing on changes that can actually happen from technical, human, and affordability standpoints.

Dr. Tinker: It's all of it. It's economics. It's technology. It's politics. It's scale. The reality is, for example, China is not going to turn back from the path it's on.

Scott mentioned that, at the time, China's five-year plan still included a lot of coal.[11] But he clarified that the plans of the United States, the United Kingdom, Germany, and India all did as well. With China and India representing one third of the entire world population, and neither country deviating from its large usage of coal, which is more than the rest of the world combined, we need to focus on real, practical solutions that can compete with what coal has to offer these countries. The most prominent attribute of coal is that it represents firm power. From the EIA, firm power is "power or power-producing capacity, intended to be available at all times during the period covered by a guaranteed commitment to deliver, even under adverse conditions."[12] Simply put, coal-generated electricity is "always on."

Dr. Tinker: You can dispatch that electricity across a grid. Natural gas can do the same, and so can nuclear. Hydro can do the same, as long as there's not a big drought. Then you start getting pretty limited in what's dispatchable. This is a challenge. Reliable energy matters to people. We like our electricity on. We've got to recognize it goes right back to the scale of demand and the kinds of energy that can provide that scale today. I think China is probably going to continue to pledge and promise, but nothing will slow them from their path to economic growth. I think they're probably thrilled to see the United States and Western Europe making all sorts of pledges like this. What does it mean? Keep sending us your manufacturing. China builds and makes over half of our stuff now. If you think that it's green, to have some other part of the world make your stuff, well, you have to ask yourself how many atmospheres are there in the globe? There's one. One. It's a pretty efficient conveyor belt up there.

As we neared the end of our conversation, Scott wanted to go back to what he sees as the most important of the three original questions he posed: Should we be doing this? Is it worth the possibility of keeping the world's temperature from rising two degrees?

Dr. Tinker: If China and India don't play, it doesn't matter. It's just too much CO_2 emissions coming for the next several decades from China and India from coal alone. If they don't do it in the next twenty to thirty years, our climate modelers tell us that we've got a big issue. I think this concept of adaptation is important, getting ready for and then not depriving those people in the world that are serious about trying to protect the environment—not just its atmosphere, but its land and air and water. We've got to show that to the world, that we are going to protect the whole environment, and we're not going to disadvantage our economy in doing it, or it will cause us not to be able to afford to do the things we need to do.

One of my favorite aphorisms is "perfect is the enemy of good." In fact, I put it as the lead quote in the introduction with credit to the French philosopher Voltaire. Certainly, the axiom applies when it comes to the energy-economy-environment triad. We need a wide path so we can make the transition work in a thousand different ways for people all around the world. Scott summed up the idea in a different way.

Dr. Tinker: We can say climate change will unfairly impact those who are poor. What will really impact them is that they don't have the energy to develop their basic needs and adapt to it like we do. We're adapting to the climate all the time in our lives. I think the world is hoping to be able to do that as well. Everybody in the world is hoping to be able to have heat in the winter and air conditioning in the summer. This is just a fundamental given in modern societies.

The good news is that technologies exist today to make that happen for all 7.8 billion people in the world, and Scott believes the first step to making this a reality is to get energy into the hands of the people who need it the most.

Dr. Tinker: That's justice. Once we begin to get that, then I think we'll be able to do things collectively in a different way.

MAGIC WAND

When asked what he would like to see happen that would have the biggest climate impact, Scott focused on educating others on energy.

Dr. Tinker: I would wave my magic wand and have everybody on Earth have a reasonable understanding of energy. I think it's the most important issue of our time.

WIDENING THE PATH

Paving the wide path requires us to accept and understand the iron law of the energy-economy-environment triad, so let's do these things:

- Watch the documentaries *Switch* and *Switch On*. Get bonus points by watching these films with a group of friends or colleagues with differing perspectives.

- Consider making a contribution to groups working to provide energy to the more than one billion people worldwide living in energy poverty. Switch Energy Alliance and Cooking for Life are two examples, but many more exist as well.

125

- An article by the *Hill* reported that, "Home energy prices are now at their highest level in more than 10 years, and, in some cases, are increasing at more than twice the rate of inflation."[13] Ask your energy provider about contributing to a local fund designed to help energy-impoverished people in your community.

CHAPTER 6

The Energy
of the Future

*Only within the moment of time represented
by the present century has one species—man—
acquired significant power to alter the nature of the world.*
— RACHEL CARSON, *MARINE BIOLOGIST,*
AUTHOR, AND CONSERVATIONIST

About 11.5 billion miles from Earth, a nuclear-powered spacecraft is working its way into interstellar space. Voyager I and Voyager II launched back in 1977.[1] Today, both continue to function thanks to a radioisotope power system about four inches by two inches in size and weighing under four pounds.[2]

Nuclear energy typically evokes fear in people not just because of the massive destruction caused by the bombing of Hiroshima and Nagasaki but also because of the devastating

127

effects of the accidents in Fukushima, Three Mile Island, and Chernobyl. Voyager I and its counterpart remind us, however, that humans have been harnessing nuclear power for good purposes for decades.

Besides fear, the biggest challenge we seem to face with nuclear power is cost. The average cost of a residential rooftop solar system now hovers around $25,000—down from about $50,000 just a decade ago.[3] Nuclear power plants, on the other hand, are between four and eight times more expensive than four decades ago. Physicist Amory Lovins once said, "Nuclear power is continuing its decades long collapse in the global marketplace because it's grossly uncompetitive . . . [and] so hopelessly uneconomic that one need not debate whether it is clean or safe."[4]

Lovins has a point, and many agree with him. That said, nuclear power is, by far, the most efficient when it comes to the materials needed to build a plant versus the amount of electricity produced.[5] By comparison, solar panels are far less efficient. Nuclear plants are much more reliable than other types of power plants.[6] They generally operate at full capacity more than 90 percent of the time, whereas coal and natural gas plants operate at full capacity just over 50 percent of the time. Even worse, wind and solar hover between 25 percent and 37 percent reliability.

Can nuclear power plants be designed to be small, safe, and cheap? For our journey to net zero to succeed, nuclear energy has to be an important part of our clean energy mix. Nuclear power, as Bill Gates puts it, "is the only carbon-free energy source that can reliably deliver power day and night, through every season, almost anywhere on earth, that [has] been proven to work on a large scale."[7]

As good as intermittent renewables and liquid fuels may be, they simply cannot fill the electricity supply gap. In the United States, the Energy Information Agency expects demand for residential power alone to increase by up to 22 percent by (you guessed it) 2050.[8]

TIME JUMP TO 2050

Here in 2050, more than 9.7 billion people share planet Earth. Since the 2020s, global energy demand has nearly doubled, with most of the growth coming from economies that developed over the first half of the century.[9] As the International Energy Agency said in its 2023 report, "A crisis with multiple dimensions requires solutions that are similarly all-encompassing."[10] Nuclear came into its own largely because intermittent power sources could not keep up with electricity demands put onto the grid by electric vehicles and heat pumps.

In the 2023 report, the organization said, "Today, low-emissions sources of electricity generation mainly include nuclear (9 percent of electricity generation) and renewables (30 percent). The share of nuclear power remains broadly stable over time in all scenarios."[11] That forecast turned out to be off by double digits. Nuclear energy took off, aided by extended reactor lifetimes; smarter permitting; a major shift in China from coal to nuclear; better and more abundant fuel stock—a wholesale switch away from, for example, uranium to thorium and sodium; and technology breakthroughs associated with fusion.[12]

Growth in the sector was also driven by the miniaturization of nuclear power plants. Innovators pushed the limits of small modular nuclear reactors to create community-scale power plants the size of a strip mall–sized convenience store—about 5,000 square feet. From a nominal capital cost of $5,500/kW in the 2020s, the cost per kW now finds itself in the $100 to $150 range.

All of this was aided by artificial intelligence, grid-optimizing quantum computing, and power-sipping super computers that consume less than 10 kW of power.[13]

Robert Bryce, Meredith Angwin, Sir Steven Cowley, Dr. Rusty Towell, Dr. Steven Koonin

Bryce • May 13, 2021 • Season 2 • episode 11

Angwin • June 22, 2021 • Season 2 • episode 13

Cowley • June 3, 2022 • Season 4 • Episode 10

Towell • June 2, 2022 • Season 4 • episode 21

Koonin • November 9, 2023 • Season 5 • episode 10

NO SUBJECT has received more attention on *Path to Zero* than nuclear energy. It's a surprise, honestly. I didn't intend for the topic to receive the airtime it has, but it is one of the happiest coincidences that has come from the podcast. Nuclear energy was top-of-mind for four guests. Robert Bryce, author, journalist, and public speaker who has been covering energy, power, innovation, and politics for more than thirty years, was the first in Season 2.[1] Chemist and author of *Shorting the Grid: The Hidden Fragility of Our Electric Grid*, Meredith Angwin, joined me just two episodes later.[2]

In Season 4, I had the pleasure of speaking with Dr. Rusty Towell, director of the Nuclear Energy eXperimental Testing (NEXT) Lab at Abilene Christian University.[3] He was also an instructor at the Naval Nuclear Power School and later earned a PhD. in nuclear physics at the University of Texas at Austin. In addition to and just before Dr. Towell, it was an extraordinary privilege to interview Sir Steven Cowley, the director of the Princeton Plasma Physics Laboratory, a US Department of Energy national laboratory for plasma physics and nuclear fusion science, who knocked my socks off in a discussion about fusion.[4] I also had the great pleasure of talking with Dr. Steven Koonin, professor at New York University, former Undersecretary for Science at the US Department of Energy in the Obama administration, and author of the book, *Unsettled: What Climate Science Tells Us, What It Doesn't, and Why it Matters.*[5]

Each of these experts had a point of view on an array of topics associated with nuclear energy. I am pleased to present portions of these conversations, each of which are key to making our net zero future possible. It is rightfully a star of the *Path to Zero* podcast. Along with emitting zero carbon, nuclear is

- firm,

- dense,

- increasingly affordable,

- safe, and

- at the cutting-edge of innovation.

Let's look at each of these ideas in turn.

Firm Energy

Firm power is electricity available at all times, even under adverse conditions.[6] In quality engineering, the expectation of firm power is akin to Six Sigma—a defect-free product 99.99966 percent of the time.[7] The "Five 9s" standard is close to the idea as well.[8] It is a measure of uptime, or how often a system is up and running, with the goal being 99.999 percent of the time. It's not an easy target to hit, and our grid doesn't really measure up. The EIA tells us that, in the United States, the average electricity customer experienced seven hours of power interruptions in 2021.[9] In that same year, Texans experienced twenty hours of outage, and Louisianans experienced an astounding eighty hours of interruption.

Ready.gov, a US government disaster preparedness website, tells us that not much good comes when the power goes out.[10] The effects are widespread and include disrupted communications, water, and transportation; closed retail businesses, grocery stores, gas stations, ATMs, banks, and other services; food spoilage and water contamination; and loss of medical device usage.

During their *Path to Zero* conversations with me, Robert Bryce and Meredith Angwin each discussed the extent to which we rely on the electric grid.

Robert: Electricity is the key to modernity. Everything we care about, all the things, nearly everything we touch, read, eat, or wear has, in some way or another, been electrified. The electric grid is the mother network; it is the network upon which all of the other networks we care about depend.

Meredith: Well, I don't think we can escape it. If we want everything to be electric . . . we had better make the electric system absolutely bulletproof, not fragile, absolutely robust. What's happening now is a hot day, a cold day. That can cause a lot of trouble that can lead to rolling blackouts. That's what I call fragility. My feeling is that, if we're trying to build everything dependent on the grid, we have to spend a lot of money to make that grid very robust. And we're actually moving in the wrong direction.

Where do we go given these expectations? Dr. Rusty Towell and

Sir Steven Cowley tackled that question during their respective *Path to Zero* episodes.

Dr. Towell: If we're not going to sit in the dark and freeze to death, what are our other options? Well, certainly, when the wind's blowing, the sun's shining, we have other options. But if we're talking about dispatchable, reliable, or on-demand energy, what are our options? Propane, fossil fuels of all sorts, or nuclear. And the only one of those sources that we've talked about that is both carbon free and dispatchable is nuclear.

Sir Cowley: We need to be able to get energy when we need it. One of the challenges of some renewables, like wind or solar, is that they are not readily available 100 percent of the time. At some point in time, there's no wind blowing, there's no sun shining. And obviously fossil does that—gas, oil, coal. But as we go to a decarbonized system, nuclear can do it.

Dense Energy

What makes these guests so sure nuclear is the way forward? Density is one of the most important reasons. Here's Robert Bryce during our *Path to Zero* conversation talking about a visit to New York's Indian Point nuclear plant in 2018.[11]

Robert: I was just stunned by the, I'll use the word *magnificence* of that plant. I mean, you had two reactors, two thousand megawatts of capacity providing a quarter of all the electricity needed by a city of eight million people—New York City—and it covered only one square kilometer on the banks of the Hudson River, forty miles north of Times Square. It was just a marvel of power density, two thousand watts per square meter.

Dr. Rusty Towell weighed in on density in his interview as well.

Dr. Towell: The lower the power density—that is the lower the amount of energy flow that you're trying to harvest—the more dilute the energy that you're trying to harvest, whether it's the photosynthetic energy of the sun, the kinetic energy of the wind, or the radiative energy of the sun. You have to counter that low power density with material inputs, more copper, more land, more concrete, more steel. And all of those things require some kind of refining and transportation, which are very carbon intensive. We don't need to have the huge investment in transmission lines running across the country from wherever your energy sources are to wherever the need is. You can bring these power supplies right next to where it is needed, whether it's the industry applications or the consumer homes. You can distribute the power supply. We no longer have to have these huge gigawatt-scale power plants with high-voltage transmission lines strung across the nation.

Affordable Energy

We're building momentum in this conversation. First, we like the idea of firm power. Now, we understand the importance of dense power. A third leg of the stool, so to speak, is affordability, and it's where Sir Steven Cowley's conversation lit the path.

Sir Cowley: Our whole civilization is based on having available energy at a cost that we can afford to use. Cost overruns in construction projects are notorious, and we've seen this in the nuclear industry. Let's make nuclear reactors essentially a factory-produced product and, therefore, make it easy to get cost reductions. The thing to remember about nuclear is that there's a huge amount of upfront investment. Fuel costs from then onward are a relatively low part of the cost of producing your electricity. If we can reduce that initial investment, we can make nuclear much more attractive to investors and to utilities.

My conversation with Dr. Steven Koonin was wide ranging, but we did touch on the nuclear conversation.

Dr. Koonin: I think in the short term, small fission reactors, small module reactors, hold a lot of promise. There are a number of companies in the West that are on the verge of actually demonstrating one of them in real operation. China is going great guns on this technology as well. We will build them in a factory, and we can come down the learning curve. I think it's a way to go and probably is the least costly way to provide reliable electricity.

On the wide path, we solve one problem, then the next. Who would have considered that between now and 2050, nuclear reactors would be prefabricated, solving the affordability problem nuclear facilities face? It's a striking idea, made even more so by the fact that it's so obvious. Firm, dense, and affordable sound like a great way forward, but just for a moment, we need to revisit that "fear" thing.

Safe Energy
Dr. Towell: This is an industry that's been around and has an extremely great safety record in the Western world. It's been used [in] hundreds and hundreds of reactors for decades and decades and decades. Obviously with any large activity, there's a certain amount of accidents. I witnessed an accident, a windmill going down the interstate near my home, where it rolled off of a shipping truck, the large parts. And so there's hazards, whether it's wind energy or nuclear power or propane, there's hazards. We have to understand those hazards and be able to do some risk analysis. We drive our cars, that's one of the most dangerous things we could possibly do. But the hazards are related to nuclear power. We have decades of experience of doing it very safely, but we can even do it better. And that's the

exciting thing to me. Water-cooled reactors can have accidents like Three Mile Island or Fukushima. No one died in either of those accidents from the radiation or reactor exposure.

Innovative Energy

Nuclear energy, we have established, is firm, dense, increasingly affordable, and safe, but is it innovative? This is where the wide path splits into three trails: extending the life of existing reactors, small modular nuclear reactors (SMNRs), and fusion reactors. Each of these trails connects back to the wide path, but each has a unique innovation story deserving attention.[12]

On extending the life of existing reactors, here are Meredith Angwin, Robert Bryce, and Sir Cowley:

Meredith: My own feeling right now is that we should be keeping our existing reactors running as long as is reasonable. We shouldn't be shutting them down because they couldn't find the missing money and the renewable plants could.

Robert: The reality is that, globally, the nuclear industry is stalled. And that's very unfortunate because I've said many times, and I'll say it again, if we're going to be serious about climate action, we have to be serious about nuclear energy.

Sir Cowley: I'm absolutely convinced that we need another generation of fission reactors, because we need to start that process of replacing fossil fuels for the long term with fission. We're going the opposite direction. We're getting fewer fission reactors in the world, and that's not going to be healthy for us. I think fission is a very important technology for the next century. Fusion will start to take over toward the end of the 2030s and the 2040s.

Sir Cowley's prediction is already coming true in the form of SMNR molten salt reactors. Per the Department of Energy, "Advanced SMRs offer many advantages, such as relatively small physical footprints, reduced capital investment, ability to be sited in locations not possible for larger nuclear plants, and provisions for incremental power additions.[13] SMRs also offer distinct safeguards, security, and nonproliferation [the prevention of more countries possessing nuclear weapons] advantages."

Rusty Towell explained SMNRs to me by saying, "We take salt, we raise the temperature, it melts, and it becomes molten salt. Now we have a fluid with great heat transfer characteristics. It is [unlike water] a fluid that never wants to become a steam, so we [avoid having a] high pressure system. What makes molten salt so much better is it can operate at high temperatures, which gives us efficiencies at low pressure, which gives us safety and decreased costs."

Molten salt technology is not a new idea. The Oak Ridge National Lab built a molten salt reactor experiment and operated it from 1965 to 1969.[14] This is one reason why startup companies like TerraPower, backed by Bill Gates, recently began testing a molten chloride fast reactor.[15] The reactor promises to produce less waste, be fully automated to reduce human error, and be built underground to protect it from attack. In addition, the technology takes us up another trail, because molten salt reactors are a category of small module reactors.

As the name implies, these are about one-third the size of traditional nuclear power plants and can be sited in a variety of locations closer to the usage point. Dow Chemical Company, for example, is incorporating SMNRs into its Seadrift manufacturing site in Texas to power the 4,700-acre campus and refining plant by the end of the decade.[16] Dow believes the project will reduce Seadrift's emissions by about 440,000 metric tons of carbon dioxide equivalent per year.

Imagine for a moment the quantum leap forward we could make in reducing carbon emissions by locating SMNRs near high energy usage points like factories, data centers, and refineries. Data centers alone account for up to 1.5 percent of electricity use worldwide and 1 percent of greenhouse gas emissions.[17] Grid fragility at a local level is improved the moment a SMNR is put into service, and because of their small size—the equipment can fit in a shipping container—rapid deployment is very possible. SMNRs have a great role to play on the path to net zero emissions.

The last trail requiring exploration in nuclear energy is fusion.

Dr. Towell: I love fusion. I think that's an amazing energy source. It has never been demonstrated that there's a commercially viable path to it. I think my favorite quote about fusion is "fusion power is forty years away and always will be." I don't think we're going to get there this decade.

He may be right, but Steven Cowley isn't letting that stop him.

Sir Cowley: It has all the benefits of being able to be turned on and turned off when you need it. It's sustainable. It's very clean. It has no accident potential that anybody should be very worried about. It's everything you would need in a perfect energy source, except it's really hard to do.

One challenge is simply temperature. Fusion reactors operate at around 150 million degrees Celsius, or ten times hotter than the center of the sun.[18]

Sir Cowley: We hold it in a cage of magnetic field, and that's much easier to do on a big scale than it is to do it on a small scale. At the moment, we need a lot of innovation to get fusion to go.

The challenge is not beyond the edge of reality anymore. In 2023, scientists at Lawrence Livermore National Laboratory's National Ignition Facility achieved net energy gain in a nuclear fusion reaction for a second time in less than a year. Fusion creates energy by merging atoms together.[19] The significance of net energy gain is that more energy is produced than is put into creating the reaction—a holy grail achievement.

It should also not go without mentioning that the core element in a fusion reactor is a type of hydrogen.

Sir Cowley: There are three types of hydrogen. There's conventional hydrogen, which has one proton in the nucleus. There's heavy hydrogen, which is in seawater. It's called deuterium, and it's one part in four thousand in seawater. There is also tritium, which is a kind of hydrogen that you have to make from lithium. There is enough of those fuels—deuterium and tritium—to power the planet for thirty million years if we extract our lithium from seawater.

Steven's *CBS Saturday Morning* interview in 2022 concluded with the fairly amazing point that we aren't that far from a cup of seawater and a couple of lithium-ion batteries, similar to the ones in your telephone, becoming the personal power source to power your life for your entire lifetime.[20]

If we had rest stops on the path to zero, it would be tempting to pull over for a moment to let those two numbers sink in: thirty million years of fuel and one cup of seawater for a lifetime of energy. We can't slow down, though. What we can do is appreciate that fusion, and SMNRs, and extending the life of existing nuclear technologies are with us today and can make a big difference in decarbonization.

Dr. Towell: Worldwide nuclear by 2050 will be the energy source that's used, whether it's large shipping containers or providing electricity or providing high process heat to industry. It'll be the number one source of energy around the globe. That's what I believe.

MAGIC WANDS

In my conversation with Sir Steven Cowley, he waved the magic wand I give to all of my guests and made an exciting wish:

Sir Cowley: I want a fusion reactor, and I want to be sitting there watching the first electricity come out of that fusion reactor. Fusion is determined by how smart you are, and I'd love to see it working as soon as possible.

Meredith: I would make sure that all nuclear power plants that are operating safely now can continue to operate for the next year and then to be extended probably for the next twenty years. And that would be the fastest change that we can have in decarbonizing our grid.

Robert: If we're going to reduce global poverty and reduce CO2 emissions, we have to be more serious and active in developing and deploying nuclear energy at the gigawatt and terawatt scale.

Dr. Towell: Let's work together to make the world a better place. We can have improved advanced nuclear; we can deploy small modular reactors rapidly. We have to improve our regulatory process. We have to have new investments. We'll need more if, by 2050, nuclear power is the dominant source of power around the globe to make safe, clean, affordable power in an environmentally friendly way without producing waste. I'd love everyone to see that vision of a better tomorrow and work to help us get there.

Just before I handed Steven Koonin his magic wand, he made a wonderful remark I think is worthy to wrap up this chapter. I asked him how he talks to his children about how they live their lives in the context of the energy transition. I appreciated his response so much I wanted to share it with you here.

Dr. Koonin: I tell them society is wonderfully adaptable and wonderful at problem solving. We will adapt as we've demonstrated we can in the past to foreseeable changes in future climates. And, at the same time, we will slowly develop effective technologies that let us gracefully reduce emissions without compromising on reliability, affordability, or providing energy to the developing world.

Be optimistic. Some of the greatest scientific minds of our time certainly are, and we should share in their enthusiasm.

WIDENING THE PATH

- Listen to one of my *Path to Zero* guests, Drew Bond, who helped us carve a wider path by giving nuclear fusion one more magic-wand wave.[21] You'll hear him say, "I'd use that wand for fusion. If we could design small fusion reactors that power large cities and countries—I mean that would just be an incredible magic wand, so I'll take that."

- Give a cheer to scientists around the world who are pursuing advancements in nuclear technologies, including Grace Stanke, a nuclear engineering student at the University of Wisconsin–Madison who was crowned Miss America 2023.[22] She is a big nuclear advocate, and I encourage everyone to listen to her perspective on the subject.

- Learn more about nuclear energy. Defeat the dread by finding something to like about it. Here are a few: carbon-free emissions, energy density, increasing affordability and safety, and some of our best energy innovations.

CHAPTER 7

Magic Wands and a Crystal Ball

Whatever you do in life, surround yourself
with smart people who'll argue with you.

—JOHN WOODEN

It's been a privilege to meet and talk with so many smart people interested in climate change and related subjects. When we first envisioned the *Path to Zero* podcast, it seemed implausible that it would become a centerpiece of engagement with others.

"What are the odds," I asked, "of people wanting to come onto a podcast and argue with me about climate change?"

As it turns out, they're very low.

Instead of arguing, my guests have brought provocative points of view and opened my eyes to a world of possibilities. I have found their counsel to be wonderfully oriented toward educating, toward thinking together, and toward finding common purpose.

Let's end on a high note.

It's with a great deal of gratitude that I close this book by honoring just a few more conversations that I enjoyed so much.

You have read that I wrap up each *Path to Zero* podcast episode by handing guests a virtual magic wand. I ask them what change they would like to see if they could wave their wand and make one big important change to the energy transition conversation in the next year. The book is peppered with more than a dozen of these responses. Here are a few more favorites:

Tisha Schuller, Principal – Adamantine Energy[1]
"I would wave that wand over a bigger tent to address climate change. My wish is that as each company sets a decarbonization or an energy future path that they're met under my imaginary negotiation tent by three environmental groups who say welcome, we're so glad you're here."

Andy Stone, *Energy Policy Now* Podcast Host and Producer – Kleinman Center for Energy[2]
"I would love to see the politics taken out of it. We have a real problem on our hands, and I understand that switching the energy system is very threatening to a lot of people. And we owe an incredible debt in this country to the people who have built our energy

system in the coal industry [and] in the oil and gas industries. At the same time, we have entered a new era, I and many believe, in which we have an existential crisis, which is climate. I would love to see the vitriol taken out of that discussion. I would like to see more discussion about how we can address this problem rationally. How can we look for a truce? How can we create opportunity, not just in the clean energy industry, but opportunities for all to take advantage of this? That's what I would like to see."

Julia Pyper, Senior Fellow – Atlantic Council[3]
"I wish there was a way to massively aggregate everyone's needs on a local level to make sure that whatever we do, whatever happens going forward, really serves the people and benefits their lives and livelihoods and their health. I feel like we get caught up in these modeling exercises and political positioning of 'what do the people really want.' I became a journalist because that's what I wanted. I wanted to help give information to people, so they can make better choices in their lives. So, I wish that there was a way that we could craft our solutions in the climate and energy space that really put people's wellbeing first."

MAGIC WANDS, MEET CRYSTAL BALL

More than they can know, I appreciate the thoughtful ways my guests have contributed to the climate change conversation with their magic wand responses. After recapping all these magic wands, I decided to turn the question on myself. If I gave myself a magic wand, what climate change–related things would I wish for?

I would wish for a crystal ball.

In my crystal ball, I would see all of the energy innovation happening today. When I look into it, I see better things ahead, and it's mostly because many of them are already happening. We are taking steps on the wide path toward a net zero future, and when we're together in 2050, we'll likely cite these among many things that got better and helped us reach our destination. Ready to give it a gaze?

BETTER FORECASTING

Humans have narrowly avoided extinction two times in history due to weather-related events.[4] The first time was around 150,000 years ago, during an ice age when the polar caps and glaciers around the world expanded, as did the deserts. The ice effectively sucked the moisture out of the atmosphere. Significant parts of central, eastern, and southeastern Africa, where all known humans lived, felt the effects. The human population at this time is estimated to have dropped below one thousand people.

The second near-extinction event was around seventy thousand years ago, following the eruption of a Sumatran volcano called Toba.[5] This wasn't just an eruption; it was a super-eruption.

Toba ejected roughly ten thousand times more ash and

gas than the 1980 Mount St. Helens eruption did and was big enough to significantly dim the sun globally for up to six years. The result was worldwide cooling and a massive dying of vegetation. This again brought the human population down, perhaps to somewhere between one thousand and five thousand people.

Granted, a volcanic eruption is not a meteorological event, but more investment in hyper-accurate weather forecasting can save a great number of lives in the aggregate over decades to come.[6] Today, a five-day forecast is about as accurate as a one-day forecast in the 1980s, so we have come a long way.

In Season 4 of the podcast, I had a great talk with Ginger Zee, chief meteorologist and managing editor of the climate unit at ABC News.[7] I'll be inviting her back soon to test the notion that, by 2050, we'll be forecasting weather down to the minute, from more than ten days away.

As the *Wall Street Journal*'s Jon Sindreu recently reported, "A golden age is dawning for climate modelers."[8] My crystal ball tells me that in the next few years, weather forecasters and meteorologists will be tracking greenhouse gas emissions on a daily basis, and we'll all be much more fluent in climate science as a result.

BETTER PAINT

The hottest color of paint in the world is super white, and it's at Purdue University.[9] Scientists there have invented, and are improving, a type of white paint that can act as a reflector, bouncing 98 percent of the sun's rays away from the earth's surface into space.

The paint scatters light and, in so doing, can make surfaces as much as 8 degrees Fahrenheit cooler than ambient air temperatures at midday, and up to 19 degrees cooler at night, reducing temperatures inside buildings and decreasing air-conditioning needs by as much as 40 percent. It is cool to the touch, even under a blazing sun, and it doesn't need any energy to work.

I don't talk enough about conservation on *Path to Zero*, so I will aim to correct that in the future. For now, I can say that, by 2050, the color of the twenty-first century will be super white. Super white buildings, and especially rooftops, will be one of our brightest climate-adaptive design standards.

BETTER GREED

This sounds weird, doesn't it? Stay with me for a moment.

I recorded an episode of *Path to Zero* entitled "2023 Predictions."[10] In that episode, I said, "The Inflation Reduction Act proved that incentives, not onerous regulations, are a great way to move toward a low carbon future." I still feel that way and want to see more incentives for low-emission solutions in critical areas like transportation, the sector responsible for nearly 40 percent of emissions.[11]

Then Dr. Wayne Winegarden came along. In our Season 4 discussion, Dr. Winegarden's comment to me was, "As opposed to saying we want to penalize the emission, because that comes with an economic cost, how can we incentivize the innovation? If you have a technology that reduces overall emissions, and obviously it needs to be defined very specifically, you can pay zero income taxes on the income that you derive from that technology."

I pair those two ideas with a fantastic magic wand provided by Jigar Shah, director of the Loan Programs Office at the US Department of Energy.[12] When Shah joined me back in Season 2, he said something that has stuck in my brain since. He waved his wand and said,

> This will be the largest wealth creation opportunity that human beings have ever seen. It will improve the lives of everyone it touches, whether it's people who move to more energy-efficient appliances, people who move to more climate-friendly transportation; whether it's all these other things. We already have all these things. But if I had a magic wand, I would move the entire conversation from "shared sacrifice" to "the greatest wealth and job-creating opportunity of our time."

I love his comment, but we appear to be moving money

in the opposite direction. In 2023, investors pulled more than $14 billion from funds that were purpose-built to support sustainability.

All of this has me believing that we need better greed.

Much of the climate change conversation feels like we are being pushed into a corner. Can we imagine creating a *pull* instead? Carbon pricing and clean investment funds may be one way to generate that pull. Government-provided incentives are yet another. I like what Rama Variankaval, global head of the center for carbon transition for JP Morgan Securities, is saying in this space. He sees decarbonization as a megatrend for global financial markets, much like digitization has been.[13] That is the scale of thinking we need, and it's why he is lining up JP Morgan to be a $2.5 trillion lender for this future. BlackRock has put a great deal of emphasis on the idea as well. In a 2022 report on managing the net zero transition, it says, "A massive reallocation of resources lies at the heart of the transition to a net-zero world."[14]

The energy transition is going to require a ton of money. The International Renewable Energy Agency believes the amount will be near $35 trillion in this decade. In whatever form it comes, the financial sector has to play a catalytic role.[15] This will entail mitigating risks, getting a reasonable return on invested capital, advising, and adopting a principled view of environmental equity. To move with urgency, perhaps Thomas Edison's perspective helps: "Opportunity is missed by most people because it is dressed in overalls and looks like work."

Good greed means our money is going to look different, it will be incentive oriented, and it will have to work harder and better than ever before.

BETTER HYDROGEN

Hydrogen is a clean and versatile fuel that produces no greenhouse gas emissions when burned.[16] It can power homes and cars, it can be used to produce fertilizer and methanol and to power hydrocracking and shipping, and it has many other applications.[17] The trouble is that it takes a lot of space to store in bulk and requires cryogenic tanks or high-pressure cylinders, which are neither convenient nor cost-effective compared to other renewable fuel sources.

The other fact about hydrogen that surprises most people is that it has to be made. Hydrogen consists of only one proton and one unpaired electron that likes to join with another electron, so hydrogen rarely floats around the world on its own.[18] You'll find it in many common places though. Water, ammonia, and even table sugar contain hydrogen. To make it, manufacturers use the steam methane method or electrolysis.[19] "Green hydrogen" uses electricity generated by wind or solar to crack apart water molecules, which requires a lot of energy—and the process is only 70–75 percent efficient.

The International Energy Agency estimates that global hydrogen production will need to be around 180 million metric tons by 2030 (from just over 90 million tons today) to reach net zero carbon emissions by 2050.[20] It's hard to do, but the speed at which better hydrogen is becoming a reality is astonishing.[21] In the future, it will be made, stored, and transported with more innovative approaches for specific applications—steel making, for example—where the energy created by hydrogen can be matched to an economy of scale.

By 2050, we'll be using hydrogen-based fuels like carbon-free ammonia at industrial scale.[22]

A 2020 Oxford Institute of Energy Studies report concluded that for large-scale, long-term energy storage, liquid ammonia is a great option and true to the wide path. Japan, Australia, the Netherlands, and the United Kingdom have national plans to use green ammonia to store (and export) their renewable energy surpluses.[23] In the United States, CF Industries—the world's current largest producer of ammonia—has begun building a green ammonia plant at Donaldsonville, Louisiana, that will produce twenty thousand tons per year when completed.

BETTER OIL

Better oil is an oxymoron, isn't it? Many experts argue that the industrial age burning of petrochemicals is the primary cause of our climate change problems. The fact is, humans have been releasing CO2 into the atmosphere by burning all manner of materials, including oil, since Paleolithic times.[24] Author Keith

Fisher documents this history in his book, *A Pipeline Runs Through It.*[25]

Burning breaks apart the hydrogen part of a hydrocarbon molecule, releasing the carbon part of the molecule along with a great deal of heat that we measure as British Thermal Units (BTUs). By 2050, we'll take it for granted that chemists have replaced the carbon backbone of the hydrocarbon molecule with heteroatoms.[26] Heteroatoms are nitrogen, oxygen, sulfur, phosphorus, chlorine, bromine, and iodine, as well as lithium and magnesium. The reason they hold the potential for better oil is that "heteroatoms enable necessary chemical diversity, reactivity, and directional bonding."[27] In other words, they make creation of a new oil possible.

You don't have to believe in this particular crystal-ball projection. You should, however, appreciate that jaw-dropping chemistry breakthroughs are happening today.

BETTER AIR

Another technology that will be commonplace by 2050 is carbon capture. Advancements in this space will make the use of petroleum a net zero proposition. This doesn't mean we won't emit carbon. It does mean, however, that the amount of carbon dioxide released into the atmosphere will be offset by the same amount removed.

In April 2022, for example, chemists from Rice University proved that used plastic, when combined with potassium acetate, is great at capturing and binding CO_2 molecules.[28] This new material, shaped into filters for power-plant stacks, promises to be several times cheaper than current methods of carbon sequestration. In 2023, the Nobel Prize in Chemistry was awarded to three scientists for their discovery of quantum dots.[29] These are nanoparticles that can be "tuned" to produce different levels of energy.

Carbon neutrality is one strategy being used today. Carbon sinks, like planting more forests to offset emissions, are a start.[30] Carbon sinks are an example of indirect capture; direct carbon capture is what we'll see in full form by 2050. Direct air capture (DAC) is among the technologies the world will scale in order to accelerate progress on the wide path.[31] It's not easy; CO_2 makes up less than 1 percent of the atmosphere, but industrial-scale air vacuums powered by wind turbines and solar panels make the prospect achievable.

BloombergNEF estimates that the global carbon market could be worth up to $1 trillion by 2037.[32] In fact, companies all over the world are racing to perfect the technology. Occidental Petroleum is planning to build more than one hundred carbon-vacuuming plants by 2035.[33] The company has secured federal funding to construct a test plant on the Gulf Coast to remove as many as a million tons of CO_2 annually. The plant is scheduled to come online in mid-2025. DACs use a lot of energy. One study estimates, "The energy needed to run direct air capture machines in 2100 [will be] up to 300 exajoules each year."[34] For comparison, the world consumed 595 exajoules of energy in 2021. DAC simply has to get better.[35]

Climeworks might have the answer. The company has raised $650 million and sold millions of dollars in CO_2 removal services.[36] The company plans to install twenty-four collector units in the next year paired with the world's largest geothermal power station in Iceland. When operational, the collector will be the biggest DAC plant in the world, capable of capturing an estimated 36,000 tons of CO_2 annually. That 36,000 tons equals just thirty seconds of the world's carbon pollution.[37]

Another astonishingly simple approach involves transforming stover, wood chips, and rice hulls—coarse plant materials often left over from harvesting—into rectangular bricks of CO_2. These plant materials are chock full of CO_2 that releases into the air as the plant materials biodegrade. A company called Graphyte has pioneered a way to turn this leftover plant material into shoebox-sized blocks, trapping the CO_2 in casted chunks for burial.[38] The company says that when maintained properly, the blocks of gas-trapping plant materials can keep CO_2 contained for a thousand years.

Is my crystal ball too foggy? It may be. One of my best guests from *Path to Zero* Season 4, Nobel Prize winner Dr. Kevin Trenberth, said, "I don't think [carbon capture] solves the problem.[39] It adds about a third to the cost of energy, so . . . the proposals being considered . . . the estimates are that it can make a very tiny dent. At the moment . . . emissions [are] 40.5 billion tons of CO2 per year, and the proposals, if you put them all together, would capture 1 million tons. So it really doesn't solve the problem, and it's incredibly expensive."

Still, I am reminded of a Winston Churchill quote. In his "Finest Hour"[40] speech on June 18, 1940, he told Parliament, "If we open a quarrel between the past and the present, we shall find that we have lost the future." My vote is to be encouraged by the present with every belief in a better future.

BETTER ELECTRICITY

In July 2020, the US Energy Information Administration published an astonishing graphic.[41] The headline above the graphic reads as follows: "More than 60 percent of energy used for electricity generation is lost in conversion." The article goes on to say that it takes 38 quadrillion BTUs (quads) of energy to produce the 14 quads of electricity we used in the United States in 2019. Thanks to natural gas combined-cycle generators, power plants are getting more efficient, but, honestly, where in the world is it okay for any system of any kind to be 40 percent efficient on average? It is clear that we need better electricity, and renewable electric generation isn't the perfect answer.

Wind power is produced by using kinetic energy to spin a turbine to generate electricity.[42] Wind energy does not emit greenhouse gases or polluting emissions, so it's good . . . but it's not great.[43] Wind is intermittent. When the wind doesn't blow, the power doesn't flow. It's also not easy to site wind turbines, as they make a lot of noise and threaten bird migrations and other wildlife. Whale deaths in the north Atlantic have been blamed on offshore wind turbines, and golden eagle populations in places like Wyoming have declined due to wind turbine bird strikes.[44]

Manufacturing wind turbines is also an energy-intensive process that emits a considerable amount of carbon. The carbon footprint of manufacturing one wind turbine is equal to 1,701 tons of CO2 equivalent.[45] Most of today's commercial turbines only achieve 45 percent efficiency, but we will likely see turbines in the future made with better technology that takes advantage of the wind when it blows.[46]

Solar panels also suffer from an efficiency problem. Residential silicon photovoltaic cells have a maximum conversion of 34 percent of photons into electrons, and the conversion rate of commercial PV panels is even less.[47] This means they don't achieve carbon neutrality until the third year of use.

Both wind and solar will help us find our way to net zero 2050. The US Energy Information Administration predicts that the combination of the two will power as much as 44 percent of the nation's grid by 2050.[48] They are going to need help, however. MIT's Energy Initiative says, "while costs have declined substantially, major scale-up in the decades ahead will depend on the solar industry's ability to overcome major hurdles with respect to cost, the availability of technology and materials to support very large-scale expansion, and successful integration at large scale into existing electric systems."[49]

One solution that will move us up the path is the grid-forming inverter. In our net zero future, we'll incorporate millions of grid-forming inverters into the 3-D grid to control the flow of intermittent electricity.[50] Inverters will smooth out the spikes that intermittent surges cause, allowing the flow of power from one part of the grid to another to maintain the sixty cycles (or Hertz) per second the grid requires to function.

Technical advances get us up the path, and there isn't enough room in this book to explore the massive changes artificial intelligence and grid-optimizing quantum computing will bring to our carbon-reducing efforts.[51] And the news gets even better. Super computers consume enormous amounts of power, some nearing thirty megawatts; quantum computers of the future will be more powerful than most supercomputers and consume less than ten kilowatts of power.

On the other hand, a nationalized energy grid won't help.[52] The permitting of large-scale transmission lines has proven to be exceptionally sticky. TransWest Express, a 732-mile transmission line, for example, took seventeen years to move from drawing board through litigation and contentious public hearings to approvals.[53] A better answer is to produce as much electricity as possible as close to the point of usage as possible, and by 2050, that's what we'll see—solar and wind energy being captured in every possible way in every possible place using ever-smaller and more efficient devices.[54] Vertical-axis wind turbines and mini solar panels will be as common as light switches.[55]

BETTER CONDUCTIVITY

Copper is an essential substance for a world that runs on electricity, and demand for new power networks, electric vehicles, and green technology is causing a massive increase in demand for the metal. The road to a net zero future, it has been reported, "begins and ends with copper."[56] Projections are that copper demand will climb more than 40 percent to 36.6 million tons by 2031, compared to the 2023 demand of roughly 25 million tons.

To keep up with this demand, the world needs to mine more copper. Mines, however, take years to develop. Of the 127 new mines opened around the world from 2002 to 2023, on average it took a mine 15.7 years to reach commercial production.[57] Companies are more likely to reopen mines that closed because of fluctuations in the price of copper, or because they became less and less viable as the ore ran thin.

That's a challenge, but copper hasn't shown us all of what it can do. By adding graphene—a highly conductive, extremely thin sheet of carbon atoms—to the manufacturing process, copper wire conductivity is improved as much as 5 percent.[58] It represents an enormous improvement considering our current grid loses around 10 percent of the power it transmits through heat loss.[59] For the US grid, this equates to dozens of nuclear power plants' worth of wasted power.[60]

By 2050, it's easy to predict that graphene-wrapped copper and other superconductive materials will be used for grid scale transmission. By using superconducting cables for key sections of the grid, we are likely to see more than efficiency benefits.[61] Superconductor lines have smaller diameters, can use smaller, less intrusive towers, and are a solution to running high-power lines in dense urban areas.[62] Astonishingly, a single seventeen-centimeter cable can carry the entire output of several nuclear plants with no heat and no lost efficiency.

The near-miraculous potential of superconductors is that they'll carry electricity over large distances with perfect efficiency. When material scientists find a way to make a conductive material work at room temperature rather than at hundreds of degrees below zero, it will revolutionize our economy and help save the environment.

BETTER BATTERIES

In 2050, we will look back and laugh at how we were storing energy in 2024. Take the example of today's EV batteries. EVs are marketed as environmental saviors. To run, however, EVs require six times the mineral input by weight of conventional vehicles, excluding steel and aluminum.[63]

Under the floor of most EVs today is an approximately 900-pound battery block containing materials like cobalt, nickel, lithium, and manganese that have been mined from the ground in far-flung places. The global supply chain that makes EV batteries possible, as is widely reported now, exacts a significant human and environmental toll.[64]

Just a few facts help illustrate the point:

- Sixty percent of the world's nickel reserves are concentrated in three countries: Indonesia, Australia, and Brazil.

- South African mines produce more than one-third of the world's manganese supply, and 70 percent of the world's cobalt is mined in the Democratic Republic of Congo. The *Washington Post* reports that more than 200,000 people work in unregulated and poorly ventilated mines.[65]

- Three of the largest current reserves for lithium are concentrated in South America's "lithium triangle," salt flats in Argentina, Bolivia, and Chile. Increased lithium demand is exhausting the region's water supply, profoundly impacting indigenous communities and the environment.[66]

The processing of these raw materials and the noxious waste left behind compounds the problems created by extraction.[67] Unfortunately, there's more bad news. It is estimated that approximately 150 million electric vehicle batteries will reach the end of their usable lives by 2035.[68] The global recycling rate of electric vehicle batteries is approximately 5 percent. The rest are stockpiled for recycling or disposed of in landfills.[69]

One of my favorite *Path to Zero* guests, Dr. Scott Tinker, had this to say about batteries:

China controls 60 percent of the world's lithium, 70 percent of the world's cobalt. They're starting to grow in their nickel. They are controlling the minerals of the future, [including] copper. So, we're moving from OPEC to China. If that makes you feel more secure, when you're talking about moving from liquids for vehicles to batteries, it's just moving the fuel source to a different region who controls it.

Toyota may have a short-term answer. It announced it has invented a solid-state battery (ceramics, not liquids, move electricity) capable of powering an electric vehicle for 745 miles on a ten-minute charge.[70] The company says that "solid-state batteries can reduce the carbon emissions of electric vehicle (EV) batteries by 39 percent." The bad news is that solid-state batteries require 35 percent more lithium than standard electric vehicle batteries.

By 2050, we'll have them at utility scale.

Sodium-ion batteries have a design similar to that of lithium-ion batteries, including a liquid electrolyte, but instead of relying on lithium, they use sodium as the main chemical ingredient. Chinese battery giant CATL is set to mass produce them by the end of 2023.[71]

Iron also holds great promise.[72] A company called Form Energy is developing an iron-air battery that uses a water-based electrolyte and basically stores energy using reversible rusting.[73] ESS corporation is building a different type of iron battery that employs similar chemistry.[74]

My bet isn't on sodium-ion or iron-air. Instead, watch for silicon, which can hold ten times as many lithium ions by weight as graphite, to bring longer-range, faster-charging, and more-affordable EVs than today's batteries.[75] As the most abundant metalloid on Earth, it will be cheaper and less susceptible to supply-chain issues.[76] Companies are already reporting record-high energy densities of up to 500 watt-hours per kilogram in silicon batteries—about twice that of today's EV batteries.[77]

When Conversations Replace Narratives

*If you're yelling, you're the one who's
lost control of the conversation.*
—TAYLOR SWIFT

The list of "better" things that will enable our net zero future could go on and on, because innovation is everywhere. Between now and 2050, we will, for example, eliminate fugitive methane emissions.[1] We'll turn plastic litter (a bane to the environment, responsible for at least 85 percent of total marine waste) into renewable propane at scale, and we'll find environmentally conscious ways to extract lithium from lake-sediment clay deposits inside dormant volcanoes.[2]

Another innovation we need is a better way to communicate with one another, which brings me to a story that I like to tell.

It was January 2021 when I learned that my *Path to Zero* production team had arranged an interview with Sarah Golden, a senior energy analyst and columnist with GreenBiz Renewable Energy Group.[3] GreenBiz is a media and events company working to accelerate the transition to a clean economy, and Sarah had caught my attention as a reporter, mostly because I wasn't sure we'd see eye to eye. At the same time, I had talked with the team about how I admired her for writing with conviction. When you read Sarah's work, you know where she stands.

I consider myself a pragmatist. Just prior to our interview, Sarah wrote an article about pragmatists versus environmentalists. I decided that would be the crux of our discussion, so when we talked, I asked her to tell me why she had written that piece. This was her response:

> This column came up for me after watching a couple of panels [at a recent conference] that were close to one another, where clean energy professionals were saying some things that sounded like they were being disparaging towards environmentalists.
>
> I heard people that really understand the scale of the climate problem and whose professions are in clean energy, definitely clean energy advocates, that made it sound like climate activists were naive or that they didn't understand how the world

worked or [that] they lacked expertise. I found it really disheartening and [felt] that dismissing of these environmentalists and climate activists is diminishing the urgency to act at a time when we really need to [be] accelerating.

I also see that having this group, that has this pure moral compass of where we need to be going, could be a really valuable tool where you're able to keep turning to them and say, "Okay, this is the speed you need us to go at. How can we go faster?" I . . . think that, in most cases, these environmentalists are right. We do need to move incredibly quickly, and it feels unreasonable sometimes because we need to move unreasonably quickly.

My interview with Sarah is recorded and posted on the *Path to Zero* webpage.[4] I encourage you to listen to it, and picture me squirming in my chair for the entire session. She pulled no punches in her assessment of fossil fuels, propane included. She was unrelenting in her call for faster action and more electrification, she questioned whether a person like me who worked for a fossil fuel derivative should even have a seat at any climate change conversation table, and at the same time she was quick and genuine, and she even took a moment to have a little fun with me.

She and I were wrestling through a question regarding

grid electric water heaters versus propane water heaters, and, after I made a smart point about the advantages of propane because of efficiency, she one-upped me by saying, "Well . . . joke's on you, 'cause I didn't shower this morning."

That was a great moment and one I'll always remember.

After we wrapped the recording, one of the production crew asked me, "Tucker, how did it feel to attend the afternoon service of the Church of the Pure Moral Compass?" *Exhausting* would have been accurate, but as I reflect on the exchange with Sarah, *grateful* is a better word. What Sarah taught me during our time together is the power and possibility of exchanging views not with the aim of changing someone else's mind, but instead for the privilege of exposing oneself to another's point of view.

Of all my *Path to Zero* podcast guests, Sarah Golden's interview holds a special place for me. She helped me become a better listener. As podcaster Scott Galloway puts it, "Listening is underrated.[5] It's a superpower. . . . [and while] we must decide what to listen to . . . many of us aren't listening, and that dampens our abilities and undermines our relationships."

I was at Climate Week in New York City in 2022, interviewing Alexander Kaufman with the *Huffington Post*.[6] We talked about electrification, nuclear energy, and other contentious issues surrounding climate change. It was a gratifying discussion in that I found myself listening with the care that Sarah Golden helped me cultivate.

What I concluded about that interview is that, while Alexander and I agree on few things, we do hold strongly to the belief that conversation, more than any technologies we may invent, is key to widening the path to net zero. I later ran across a great article he wrote, containing this passage:

> On a national level, members of both US parties are trying to make it easier to build energy infrastructure like new transmission lines as well as wind turbines and solar panels. On a local level, town halls and county legislatures are often trying to throw up as many impediments as possible to upgrade or install new infrastructure. A 2018 survey of counties by the National Renewable Energy Laboratory found 286 regulations in 105 municipalities on wind turbines. When they did the survey again in 2022, that jumped to 461 municipalities, averaging four ordinances per jurisdiction, with a spike to 315 municipalities that tried to prevent solar panels.

How is it that we can mostly agree on the idea that climate change poses an existential threat to the planet, but we behave differently when it comes time to act? The book, *Change is Good . . . You Go First*, by Mac Anderson and Tom Feltenstein, pops into my head whenever I see the failure of talk to translate into walk.[7]

NIMBY (not in my back yard), CAVE (citizens against virtually everything), BANANAs (build absolutely nothing anywhere near anyone), and a dozen other acronyms describe the effect we have on one another when talking grinds up against taking action. We often hear of support for renewable energy, for example, but surveys show that people are less enthusiastic about having it nearby.[8] One found that only 24 percent of Americans were willing to live within a mile of a solar farm. The number dropped to 17 percent for wind farms.

Agrivoltaics, using land for both agriculture and solar generation, may provide a way to widen the path.[9] As Dr. Katharine Hayhoe pointed out in her 2020 interview with us, "If Texas wanted to supply the whole US with electricity, all you would need is a hundred by a hundred square miles covered in solar panels, and that would be enough energy for the whole country."[10]

But even in Texas, the renewable energy center of the country in many respects, people aren't in a welcoming mood.[11] Opponents argue that wind and solar projects kill birds and bats, and solar farms take away too much land.

To my earlier list of better things we need, then, let me add that we need a better way to disagree with one another. In this context, I like what Tilak Doshi told me in the very first season of *Path to Zero*: "Let the disinfectant of open debate drive off bad ideas and bring in good ideas."

He's right.

Many of the arguments we have about climate change today have been dragging on for too long. Some Gen Xers, Millennials, and Gen Zers seem resigned to doomerism about their futures, largely because of climate change and the lack of optimism surrounding the subject. We owe them more.

Let's argue better by not arguing about whether climate change is real, whether it's driven by humans or natural cycles, or whether it's a serious problem. Let's instead debate how to do more, not how to do less. And let's debate with the optimism that, whatever answer we land on, we can and will make it work.

I am reminded by a recent *Scientific American* article about how we solved the terrible problem of acid rain, which was once thought to be a lost cause.[12] And how about this: Did you know that the hole in the ozone layer, first raised as a major issue in the early 1980s, has closed dramatically?[13] That's right. It is now close to a complete recovery.

Evolutionary biologists Joseph Henrich and Michael Muthukrishna help us with this issue. In their work, they describe humans as "ultrasocial," meaning we "cooperate more than other mammals both at small scales . . . and at larger scales."[14] I am encouraged that many hands, as the saying goes, can indeed make light work.[15] As long as the journey ahead may be, my commitment is to keep the conversation going.

TIME JUMP TO 2050

Here in 2050, historians agree that it was human connection, more than any technological advancement, that made net zero a reality. The conversations recounted in this book were just the tip of the iceberg.

The millions of conversations that changed the world started in living rooms and bars and echoed in the halls of local and state governments. Climate imperatives began to align with human energy needs. Narratives were toppled and replaced with constructive dialogue based on shared understanding and mutual respect. Once that happened, world leadership adapted to reflect the spirit of cooperation sweeping the planet.

This all may seem far-fetched, but I would argue it's no less fanciful than some of the narrow solutions on the table in 2024. It starts with the simple act of sitting down and talking with someone who may have a different point of view. The year 2050 will be here before you know it, so you'd better get started.

Acknowledgments

Hope is the happy feeling that comes with the expectation and desire that an abstraction will become a reality. Many people supported me in making this book a reality, and for that I am thankful. You provide me with hope that putting my views onto these pages could inspire others to harness the better angels of human nature.

In climate change, we face the most complex challenge humankind has ever confronted. My hope is that we face this challenge together, united by a determination to act rationally and in concert to make the world better.

A special thanks to my *Path to Zero* guests. The conversations and connections made through the show have been a great privilege.

Also, much gratitude goes to my colleagues, friends, and mentors at the Propane Education & Research Council, to its board of directors, and to the team at Hahn Public, who produced the *Path to Zero* podcast.

I would like to thank my wife, Liz, for her patience and encouragement throughout the writing of this book. Without her support, I would never have been able to tackle this project.

Thank you all for your persistent encouragement and generous infusions of optimism, often at just the right times.

PATH TO ZERO
Episodes by Season

SEASON 5 EPISODES (24)

5.24 – Driving Innovation to Decarbonize Utilities with Emerson's Robert Yeager. Tucker discusses the key drivers behind the decarbonization of power with the president of Power and Water Solutions for Emerson at the Reuters Energy Transition Summit in Houston.

5.23 – Turning Flared Methane into Computing Power with Chase Lochmiller, CEO of Crusoe Energy. Tucker talks about climate innovation with the founder of an energy technology company that captures stranded energy (gas flaring) to power modular data centers.

5.22 – Using Oil and Gas Infrastructure for Alternate Energy Sources with Cindy Taff, CEO of Sage Geosystems. At the Reuters Energy Transition Summit in Houston, *Path to Zero* caught up with Cindy Taff to discuss how geothermal systems are poised to make a huge impact on climate change.

5.21 – The Electric Sector's Efforts to Decarbonize and Enhance Resiliency with Emily Fisher, Senior Vice President, Edison Electric Institute. The trade association that represents all US investor-owned electric companies is working to accelerate the development of clean energy technologies.

5.20 – Home Automation as a Power Resilience and Decarbonization Tool with Bob Madonna, CEO of Savant Systems. We continued our Reuters Energy Transition Summit episodes by speaking with Bob Madonna about the smart energy revolution he envisions and how the grid can keep up with increasing electrification demands.

5.19 – Groundbreaking Solar Thermal Technology with Christie Obiaya, CEO at Heliogen. Tucker talks to the leader of a company that is a great example of how innovation is addressing the challenge of decarbonization. Heliogen combines solar thermal technology with artificial intelligence and thermal energy storage.

5.18 – Grid Reliability and the Future of Renewables with Ed Hirs, Energy Fellow at the University of Houston, Division of Energy and Innovation. Tucker and Ed discuss the Biden administration's climate goals, the Texas Legislature's response to Winter Storm Uri, and the future of the Texas grid.

5.17 – The Importance of Considering the Environmental Lifecycle with Rachel A. Meidl, Energy and Environment Fellow, Rice Baker Institute for Public Policy. At the Reuters Energy Transition Summit, Dr. Meidl talked to Tucker about how to think about carbon in a different way and the risk of omitting hazardous waste and equity from climate change discussions.

5.16 – How Climate Change is Exacerbating Environmental Justice with Dr. Robert Bullard, the Father of Environmental Justice, and Distinguished Professor at Texas Southern University. Dr. Bullard discusses the history of the environmental justice movement and how to ensure our climate policies are equitable for generations to come.

5.15 – How to Prepare for Climate Change with David Pogue, CBS News Sunday Morning Correspondent reporting on Tech, Science, and Environment. During Climate Week New York, Tucker had the honor of speaking with esteemed journalist David Pogue about his fascinating career and why we should be focused on adaptation to climate change versus just mitigation.

5.14 – Bringing Access to Clean Energy in Developing Countries with James Rockall, CEO, World LP Gas Association. Rockwall talks to Tucker about propane's contributions toward improved indoor and outdoor air quality and reduced greenhouse gas emissions.

5.13 – Decarbonizing the Transportation Sector with Dr. Rachel Muncrief, Acting Executive Director, International Council on Clean Transportation. Dr. Muncrief talks to Tucker about how the ICTT is taking on the complex topic of decarbonizing some of the most difficult industries: heavy-duty trucking, shipping, and air travel.

5.12 – How ESG Principles are Reshaping Capital with Silvia Pavoni, Founder and Editor, Financial Times Sustainable Views. At our Climate Week studio, we sat down with Silvia Pavoni to discuss how global environmental, social, and governance policies and regulations are driving changes in investment portfolios.

5.11 – Columbia Climate School's Dr. Steven Cohen on how we solve our environmental problems without destroying the economy. Dr. Cohen is the author of *Environmentally Sustainable Growth: A Pragmatic Approach*.

5.10 – A Closer Look at Climate Data with Theoretical Physicist Dr. Steven Koonin. Tucker talks to the former undersecretary for science at the US Department of Energy in the Obama administration about his book, *Unsettled: What Climate Science Tells Us, What It Doesn't, and Why It Matters*.

5.09 – NYU Research Professor Amy Myers Jaffe on Curbing Climate Change with Digital Technologies. In his series of interviews from Climate Week in New York City, Tucker looks at the role of technological change in altering the global energy system with a true thought leader on global energy policy and sustainability.

5.08 – Sustained Investment to Avoid a Climate Catastrophe with Columbia University's Bruce Usher. Tucker continues his series of conversations from Climate Week in New York City with a fascinating discussion with climate finance expert Bruce Usher, who is part of the faculty at both the Columbia Business School and Climate School.

5.07 – Transforming Our Global Energy System with Cipher's Amy Harder. Tucker kicks off a series of special episodes recorded at Climate Week in New York City with one of the nation's premier climate journalists. Amy Harder is the executive editor of Cipher, which covers the technological innovations we need to combat climate change and transform our global energy systems.

5.06 – Special *Path to Zero* Event for Climate Week NYC. We invite you to watch this special *Path to Zero* event featuring NYC's Chief Fleet Officer and innovators in renewable fuels and carbon recycling technology.

5.05 – A Turning Point for Carbon Capture and Storage (CCS) with Geologist Dr. Tip Meckel. Carbon capture and storage (CCS) is currently the biggest hammer in the toolbox for reducing significant amounts of industrial emissions, according to our guest in this special episode of *Path to Zero*.

5.04 – NBC News Climate Unit Journalist Carlos P. Beltran on Humanizing the Climate Change Story. *Path to Zero* continues its series of episodes recorded from the Reuters Global Energy Transition Summit in New York with a special guest, Carlos P. Beltran, a producer with the climate unit at NBC News.

5.03 – Industry Decarbonization Through Automation with Emerson CTO Peter Zornio. At the Reuters Global Energy Transition Summit, *Path to Zero* was fortunate to visit one of the innovators in decarbonizing the industrial sector, Peter Zornio, Chief Technology Officer at Emerson. He leads innovation strategy and R&D for the global technology, software, and automation leader.

5.02 – NBC News Science Reporter Denise Chow on Wildfire Smoke and other Climate Change Weather Extremes. *Path to Zero* continues its series of episodes recorded from the Reuters Global Energy Transition Summit in New York with a special guest, Denise Chow, who reports on science and climate change for NBC News.

5.01 – Climate Change Adaptation with Columbia Climate School's Dr. Lisa Dale. Tucker kicks off a series of special episodes recorded from the Reuters Global Energy Transition Summit in New York by welcoming Dr. Lisa Dale, an expert on climate change adaptation from the Columbia University Climate School.

SEASON 4 EPISODES (21)

4.21 – Could Molten Salt Reactors Boost Nuclear Energy? A conversation with Dr. Rusty Towell, Nuclear Researcher and Physics Professor at Abilene Christian University. In this episode, *Path to Zero* explores molten salt nuclear technology with an innovator who is heading up research that he believes will lead to safer, cleaner, and more affordable nuclear power.

4.20 – Climate Change Water Resilience with Journalist Erica Gies. *Path to Zero* takes an in-depth look at the Slow Water Movement with the journalist who coined the phrase, Erica Gies.

4.19 – Citizen's Guide to Combat Climate Change with Energy Policy Expert Hal Harvey. In this episode, Tucker talks with acclaimed energy policy advisor Hal Harvey, who says individuals can make a difference and has a new book that is a citizen's guide on how you can combat climate change.

4.18 – Climate Scientist Kevin Trenberth on Making the Biggest Difference with Climate Change. *Path to Zero* recognizes Earth Day 2023 with an objective assessment on where things stand regarding the fight against climate change and the planet's weather patterns with Dr. Kevin Trenberth, one of the world's premier climate scientists.

4.17 – The Pathway to Green Shipping with Green Marine's Eleanor Kirtley. Tucker continues his look at efforts to decarbonize transportation in a conversation with the largest voluntary environmental certification program for the maritime industry in North America. Dr. Eleanor Kirtley is a senior program manager for Green Marine, which works with ports, ship operators, terminals, and others to help improve their environmental performance.

4.16 – The Decarbonization of Trucking with NACFE's Mike Roeth. In this episode, Tucker has the opportunity to talk to Mike Roeth, who is one of the leading authorities on enhancing the efficiency and decarbonization of the trucking industry. Mike has been the executive director of North American Council for Freight Efficiency since 2010.

4.15 – The *New Yorker*'s Elizabeth Kolbert on the Unintended Consequences of Human Interventions in the Natural World. In this episode, Tucker has the opportunity to talk to one of the foremost writers on climate change and the state of the earth.

4.14 – Global Clean Energy's Richard Palmer on Camelina: Is It the Wonder Crop for Renewable Fuels? This episode features a deep discussion on the game-changing crop, Camelina, which is quickly becoming a popular feedstock for renewable fuels production. Tucker welcomes the head of the world's leading developer of camelina. Richard Palmer is CEO of Global Clean Energy, which owns Sustainable Oils, a camelina breeding and production businesses in the United States. Global Clean Energy also owns the largest camelina company in Europe, Camelina Company España S. L.

4.13 – Decarbonizing the Nation's Ports with Ian Gansler of the American Association of Port Authorities. In this episode, we have an opportunity to talk to Ian Gansler, who is heading up a bold new program for the American Association of Port Authorities (AAPA) to meet the twin challenges of energy security and climate change.

4.12 – Hydrogen: Hope or Hype? with Author John Armstrong. This episode of *Path to Zero* is all about hydrogen. The energy is viewed by many to be *the* energy answer to climate change and the surest path to net zero carbon emissions. Our guest is an energy expert who is going to help us dig into the future challenges and opportunities with hydrogen.

4.11 – 2023 Energy Predictions. It's a special edition of *Path to Zero* where Tucker looks into his crystal ball for 2023 as it pertains to energy. He explores five big energy topics and what he sees for the year ahead.

4.10 – Making Nuclear Fusion a Successful Power Source with Princeton's Sir Steven Cowley. Fusion has held a great deal of promise for decades to potentially generate carbon-free electricity. Some leaders believe we are at a turning point for fusion-powered energy.

4.09 – The Future of EV Batteries with Battery Expert Bob Galyen. In this episode of *Path to Zero*, Tucker has an opportunity to talk to one of the most respected experts in the battery world. Bob Galyen was the lead battery engineer on the EV1, General Motors's first mass-produced electric car that debuted in 1996.

4.08 – Market-Oriented Solutions to Climate Change with Pacific Research Institute's Dr. Wayne Winegarden. Can free market solutions help combat climate change? Our guest in this episode is an economist who studies the connection between macroeconomic policies and economic outcomes, with a particular focus on the energy sector.

4.07 – *Wall Street Journal's* Amrith Ramkumar on Financing the Clean Energy Transition. There's no doubt the financial markets are going to have a big impact in the fight against climate change. Our guest in this episode of *Path to Zero* covers how investors are financing the transition to clean energy. Amrith Ramkumar is the climate finance reporter for the *Wall Street Journal*.

4.06 – The Push to Net-Zero Carbon Transport with World Energy's Gary Grimes. In this episode, Tucker visits with the director of sustainability for liquid fuels innovator World

Energy. Gary Grimes is playing a key role in the huge investment the company is making in a new biofuel and hydrogen production facility in Southern California.

4.05 – Challenging Prevailing Climate Change Narratives with *HuffPost*'s Alexander Kaufman. Tucker welcomes the award-winning senior reporter at *HuffPost*, Alexander Kaufman, to *Path to Zero*'s special Climate Week episodes in New York City. The two discuss electrification, nuclear energy, and many other contentious issues surrounding climate change.

4.04 – Energy Transition Impact on Capital Markets with Carbon Tracker's Rob Schuwerk. How economic factors can affect climate change is the focus of this special episode of *Path to Zero* from Climate Week in New York City. Tucker welcomes Rob Schuwerk, North American Executive Director of Carbon Tracker, who was in New York to launch the first ever Global Registry of Fossil Fuels.

4.03 – Environmental Justice and Climate Change with Insider's Catherine Boudreau. *Path to Zero*'s special episodes from New York for Climate Week continue with Catherine Boudreau, the senior sustainability reporter at Insider. She's in New York covering Climate Week and stopped by to join *Path to Zero*.

4.02 – ABC News Meteorologist Ginger Zee Talks Conservation and Climate. *Path to Zero*'s special Climate Week conversations from New York continue with a visit from ABC News's climate unit and chief meteorologist Ginger Zee.

4.01 – Climate Week Special with *Vox's Future Perfect* Editor Bryan Walsh. *Path to Zero* is on the road for a series of special episodes in New York City for Climate Week. We kick things off with journalist Bryan Walsh, who runs the *Future Perfect* section at *Vox*, which focuses on emerging technology, tech ethics, and how to make the future a better place.

SEASON 3 EPISODES (17)

3.17 – Renewable Fuels and the Fight Against Climate Change with Renewable Energy Group's Kevin Lucke. In this episode of *Path to Zero*, Tucker continues the conversation on how renewable fuels can help address the carbon emissions challenge.

3.16 – The Physics of Climate Change with Dr. Lawrence Krauss. Joining Tucker in this edition of *Path to Zero* is internationally known theoretical physicist and best-selling author Dr. Lawrence Krauss. He's known for presenting the most accurate scientific information in a way that is accessible to laypeople.

3.15 – Reducing Carbon Intensity with Renewable Propane. In a special edition of *Path to Zero*, Tucker Perkins shares some significant news about renewable propane and why it's a clean energy breakthrough.

3.14 – The Many Paths to Decarbonization with Southwest Research Institute's Dr. Graham Conway. Keeping all options open to decarbonize, not just the all-electric route, is the view of our guest in this episode of *Path to Zero*.

3.13 – Climate Disaster Preparedness with Columbia's Jeffrey Schlegelmilch. In a far-reaching conversation, Tucker covers climate disaster preparedness, microgrids, and grid resiliency with Jeffrey Schlegelmilch, Research Scholar and Director of the National Center for Disaster Preparedness at Columbia University's Earth Institute.

3.12 – Agricultural Innovations That Help Curtail Climate Change. In this episode of *Path to Zero*, our focus is on technological advancements in agriculture that are helping farmers cut or eliminate the use of harmful chemicals, as well as reduce carbon emissions.

3.11 – Alternate Routes on the Road to Zero Emissions, Part 2. Achieving sustainable mobility will require multiple solutions, according to two experts in automotive engineering who talk to Tucker in the second of a two-part episode of *Path to Zero*.

3.10 – The Fastest Way to Driving Green, Part 1. Two experts on automotive engineering join Tucker to share a realistic take on achieving sustainable mobility. Oxford engineering professor Felix Leach and Kelly Senecal, cofounder of Convergent Science, are the authors of the book *Racing Toward Zero: The Untold Story of Driving Green*. The book is a 2022 Independent Press Award winner.

3.09 – Midstream Industry Looks to "Clear the Air" to Support Energy Transition. This episode of *Path to Zero* focuses on how an important industry is navigating the energy transition to tackle the environmental challenges we face.

3.08 – The Human Toll of Climate Change with *Financial Times's Moral Money* Editor Simon Mundy. Tucker's guest in this episode is *Financial Times* journalist and editor of *Moral Money*, Simon Mundy, to talk about the challenges of climate change in an up-close and personal way.

3.07 – Waving a Magic Wand to Slow Climate Change. If some of the world's leading climate experts were given a magic wand to change one thing to make the biggest impact with climate change, what would they do? We find out in this special episode as Tucker looks back on some of the more memorable comments by *Path to Zero* guests.

3.06 – New Decarbonizing Truck Engine Technology with Fleet Operations Expert Kevin Hahn. In this episode of *Path to Zero*, Tucker gets the perspective of a veteran fleet manager on the potential of recently unveiled truck engine technology designed to help fleet owners decarbonize today.

3.05 – Designing Homes to Withstand Climate Change Fueled Disasters with Author Boyce Thompson. Resilient home design is the subject of this episode as Tucker speaks to journalist Boyce Thompson, author of the book *Designing for Disaster*.

3.04 – Ocean-Based Carbon Removal with Northwestern University's Dr. Wil Burns. Developing methods to enhance ocean-based carbon dioxide removal is one of the topics Tucker explores with an expert who has been studying climate change for more than thirty years.

3.03 – Finding Climate Change Hope with Dr. Katharine Hayhoe. In this episode, Tucker has the privilege of talking to a preeminent climate scientist whom the *New York Times* described as "one of the nation's most effective communicators on climate change."

3.02 – The *Wall Street Journal's* Elizabeth Findell on the Texas Winter Storm and Grid Failure – One Year Later. In this episode, *Wall Street Journal* reporter Elizabeth Findell reflects on the one-year anniversary of the devastating winter storm known as Uri. It brought record cold and ice to the Southwest and caused the Texas electric grid to fail.

3.01 – Renewable Fuels Innovation. Tucker kicks off Season 3 of *Path to Zero* by talking to Nik Weinberg-Lynn, who is heading up a project to create one of the largest renewable fuel plants in the world.

SEASON 2 EPISODES (21)

2.21 – The Science, Policy, and Economics of Decarbonization. In a far-reaching conversation, Dr. Paltsev talks to Tucker about the outcomes of the Glasgow summit, coordinated action to decarbonize the planet, financial risks associated with climate change, and the different types of energy needed to stabilize the climate.

2.20 – Transportation Decarbonization. In this episode, Tucker welcomes an expert in transportation decarbonization and policy. Mollie Cohen D'Agostino is policy director for the 3 Revolutions Future Mobility Program at the Institute of Transportation Studies at the University of California, Davis.

2.19 – Accelerating Energy Innovation to Mitigate Climate Change. In this episode, Tucker talks to Drew Bond, former senior advisor to President George W. Bush at the Department of Energy and cofounder of C3 Solutions, a non-profit organization committed to free-market solutions for climate change.

2.18 – Propane as a Tool for Decarbonization. This is the first episode of *Path to Zero* recorded in front of a live audience at the National Association of State Energy Officials (NASEO) annual conference in Portland, Maine. Tucker turns over his hosting duties to Alan Zelenka, an Oregon energy official, to be interviewed about how propane can be a tool to help states meet decarbonization goals.

2.17 – Designing Zero Net Energy Homes. Zero Net Energy (ZNE) homes are starting to shake up the US housing market. Tucker's conversation in this edition of *Path to Zero* is with David Knight, an expert on designing ZNE homes who has been a leader in green building for nearly forty years.

2.16 – Sustainable Alternatives for the Outdoors, Part 2. In the second of a two-part episode focused on sustainable solutions that help create a wider path to net zero emissions, Tucker Perkins welcomes Josh Simpson with Little Kamper. The California company has developed an innovative product that is helping keep hazardous waste out of our parks.

2.15 – Sustainable Alternatives for the Outdoors, Part 1. In this episode, outdoor industry executive and Arctic adventurer Graeme Esarey joins Tucker in the first of a two-part episode focused on innovative solutions that help us get to net zero emissions.

2.14 – DOE's Jigar Shah on Financing Clean Energy Projects. In this episode, the focus is on the U.S Department of Energy's efforts to roll out billions of dollars in grants to stimulate the transition to a clean energy economy.

2.13 – Climate Change and Electric Grid Resiliency. In this episode, Tucker welcomes chemist and energy analyst Meredith Angwin, who has written an eye-opening exposé about the vulnerabilities of our electric grid.

2.12 – Energy Transition Complexities with Geologist Dr. Scott Tinker. In this episode of *Path to Zero*, Tucker explores the challenges of the global energy transition with an expert who has been working for years on educating the public that every energy source has pros and cons, and sustainability will require an energy mix.

2.11 – Is Nuclear Power the Path to Low-Carbon Energy? Nuclear energy is just one of the topics covered in this episode, in which Tucker turns the tables on a fellow energy podcast host, Robert Bryce.

2.10 – Accelerating Decarbonization with Microgrids. Tucker talks to an energy industry leader whose expertise in microgrids and renewable energy goes back more than four decades.

2.09 – Cyberattack Threats to the Nation's Critical Energy Infrastructure. This episode of *Path to Zero* is particularly timely with the recent cyberattack that shut down a major oil pipeline.

2.08 – Earth Day Special: The Best of the Magic Wand Question. Tucker celebrates Earth Day by waving a magic wand on the one thing that will make the biggest difference to get to a zero emissions future.

2.07 – Can Fossil Fuels Help Address Climate Change? Energy consultant and author Tisha Schuller joins Tucker for a fascinating discussion on how addressing climate change happens better, faster, and cheaper with the oil and gas industry at the table.

2.06 – Racial Disparities and Climate Change. Environmental justice takes center stage once again on *Path to Zero* as Tucker Perkins welcomes a special guest who has worked for more than a decade to address the many practices that are harming communities of color nationwide. Jacqueline Patterson is the senior director of the Environmental and Climate Justice Program at the NAACP.

2.05 – Carbon Removal with Dr. Sabine Fuss, Mercator Research Institute. Carbon removal is the subject of this episode, and Tucker welcomes one of the world's leading experts on the subject to bring us up to speed on the technological advances happening in this part of the climate change conversation.

2.04 – Propane Patio Heaters or Fire Pits? Which is Better for the Environment? Tucker Perkins welcomes a leading fire scientist to get some insight on the chemistry of carbon related to patio heaters.

2.03 – Do fossil fuel interests deserve a seat at the table? In this special episode of *Path to Zero*, host Tucker Perkins has a no-holds-barred conversation with Sarah Golden, Senior Energy Analyst with GreenBiz Group.

2.02 – Are Microgrids the Answer to a Cleaner, More Resilient Electric Grid? A cleaner electric grid is seen is a key element to reducing carbon in the atmosphere. Interest in microgrids is growing because of their ability to incorporate renewable and low carbon energy sources, as well as sustain electricity service during natural disasters.

2.01 – Climate Policy Shift with Greentech Media's Julia Pyper. Tucker kicks off the new year and a new season of *Path to Zero* by talking to a journalist and podcast host who has some amazing perspective on climate policy and what we can expect with the changes in Washington.

SEASON 1 EPISODES (16)

1.16 – 5 Energy Trends and Predictions for 2021. To kick off 2021, Tucker Perkins reflects on some memorable moments from the conversations with energy experts on *Path to Zero* to look ahead to the big clean energy trends over the next year.

1.15 – Top 5 Energy Policy Changes to Expect in Biden's Presidency. *Path to Zero* concludes Season 1 by hearing from a foremost expert on energy policy about carbon pricing, energy storage, and the big changes coming in 2021 with the new administration. Andy Stone is host and producer of the Energy Policy Now podcast with the Kleinman Center for Energy Policy at the University of Pennsylvania.

1.14 – Can Digitalization Solve the Carbon Crisis? In this episode of *Path to Zero*, host Tucker Perkins invites renewable energy expert Mathias Steck to discuss technology's role in carbon reduction with cleaner, greener energy.

1.13 – How Oil-Pumping Texas Became the Leader in Wind Power. In this episode of *Path to Zero*, Tucker talks to Asher Price, a journalist and author who has reported on the rapid rise of wind in the state that is one of the largest wind generators in the world. In Texas, wind accounts for about 20 percent of the state's electricity.

1.12 – Dr. Tilak Doshi, *Forbes* Energy Contributor. In this episode of *Path to Zero*, host Tucker Perkins welcomes Dr. Tilak Doshi, *Forbes* energy contributor and Muse, Stancil & Company managing consultant for Asia.

1.11 – Ken Silverstein, *Forbes* Energy Contributor. In this episode of *Path to Zero*, host Tucker Perkins talks with Ken Silverstein, a senior energy contributor at *Forbes*, about the future of micro-grids and other advancements in the energy industry.

1.10 – Resiliency Part 2: World Central Kitchen. In the second of a special two-part episode focused on resiliency, Tucker Perkins speaks with Alexandra Garcia, Chief Program Officer with World Central Kitchen (WCK).

1.09 – Resiliency Part 1: The Healing Power of BBQ. In the first of a special two-part episode focused on resiliency, Tucker Perkins speaks with Stan Hays, cofounder of Operation BBQ Relief (OBR) and 2017 CNN Hero.

1.08 – Could Propane be the New Diesel? In this episode of *Path to Zero*, host Tucker Perkins invites Dr. Bryan Wilson, the executive director of the Energy Institute at Colorado State University (CSU), and Dr. Daniel Olsen, a mechanical engineering professor at CSU, to provide an in-depth look into the recent $3.5 million US Department of Energy (DOE) grant awarded to the university for the development of new, high-efficiency propane engines.

1.07 – Human Behavior and a Recipe for a Low Carbon Future. In this episode of *Path to Zero*, host Tucker Perkins speaks with Dr. Joshua Rhodes, a research fellow at the Energy Institute and the Webber Energy Group at the University of Texas at Austin, about a seven-step recipe to achieve low carbon energy, the implications of the electrification movement, and the recent rolling blackouts in California.

1.06 – Renewable Propane as the Fuel of the Future. In this episode of *Path to Zero*, host Tucker Perkins welcomes Joy Alafia, the president and CEO of the Western Propane Gas Association, to discuss renewable propane as the clean and sustainable fuel of the future.

1.05 – Renewable Gases. In this episode of *Path to Zero*, we discuss the benefits of renewable gases to move society closer to a low carbon, low emission future. Host Tucker Perkins welcomes Cliff Gladstein, the founding president of GNA, a clean transportation and energy consulting firm. Gladstein provides an in-depth look behind his latest webinar series, *Renewable Gas 360*.

1.04 – Developing Climate Change Positive Communities. *Path to Zero* host Tucker Perkins welcomes the partners behind an initiative to develop sustainable, planned villages capable of reducing the carbon footprint of a community by ten times. Patrick Van Haren and Karin Aston are the cofounders of Citadels, a new-generation development company combining traditional neighborhood design with regenerative agriculture to create distinctive master-planned communities.

1.03 – Environmental Justice Part 2: Where the Movement Stands Now in the Age of COVID-19 and BLM. In the second of a two-part series on environmental justice, Tucker Perkins speaks with author and department chair of environmental studies at University of California in Santa Barbara, Dr. David Pellow, about the difficulty of reaching environmental sustainability in areas with marginalized populations.

1.02 – Environmental Justice: What Is It and Why Is It So Important? In the first of a two-part series on environmental justice, Tucker Perkins speaks with law professor Alice Kaswan about how pollution negatively impacts marginalized communities.

1.01 – A Stake in the Ground. Host Tucker Perkins kicks off the premiere episode of *Path to Zero* with a discussion on a practical path toward a zero emissions future for our country and world. Tucker's guest is Daniel Dixon, the incoming chair of the Propane Education & Research Council.

Notes

INTRODUCTION

1. Hiroko Tabuchi, "The New Soldiers in Propane's Fight Against Climate Action: Television Stars," *New York Times*, January 12, 2023, https://www.nytimes.com/2023/01/11/climate/climate-propane -influence-campaign.html.

2. Chef Charlie, "Enjoy the Ride!" *Epicurean Global Exchange* (blog), September 16, 2021, https://epicureanglobalexchange.com/enjoy -the-ride/.

3. Matthew Schaefer, "H. L. Mencken: Sage of Baltimore," *Hoover Heads* (blog), Herbert Hoover Library and Museum, October 16, 2019, https://hoover.blogs.archives.gov/2019/10/16/h-l-mencken-sage -of-baltimore/.

CHAPTER 1

1. Tsuyoshi Inajima, "Toyota Keeps Title as No. 1 Carmaker for Third Straight Year," *Bloomberg*, January 29, 2023, https://www.bloomberg. com/news/articles/2023-01-30/toyota-keeps-title-as-no-1-carmaker -for-third-straight-year#xj4y7vzkg.

2. Dan Avery, "Which States Have the Most EV Charging Stations?" *CNET*, March 17, 2023, https://www.cnet.com/roadshow/news /how-many-ev-charging-stations-are-there-in-the-us/.

3. US Department of Energy, "Number of Gasoline Stations, 1994-2004," accessed November 12, 2023, https://www.fueleconomy.gov /feg/quizzes/answerquiz16.shtml; Joe Thomas, "How Many Chargers Per Electric Vehicle Charging Station?" *Medium,* July 15, 2021, https://medium.com/predict/how-many-chargers-per-electric-vehicle -charging-station-5bd253e4dd60.

4. Vanessa Peng, "How Much Does a Commercial EV Charging Station Cost?" *Watt Logic* (blog), July 26, 2022, https://wattlogic.com/blog /commercial-ev-charging-stations-cost/.

NOTES

5. The White House, "Fact Sheet: Biden-Harris Administration Announces New Standards and Major Progress for a Made-in-America National Network of Electric Vehicle Chargers," accessed November 12, 2023, https://www.whitehouse.gov/briefing-room/statements-releases/2023/02/15/fact-sheet-biden-harris-administration-announces-new-standards-and-major-progress-for-a-made-in-america-national-network-of-electric-vehicle-chargers/.

6. Steven Loveday, "How Long Does It Take to Charge an Electric Car?" *US News and World Report*, April 19, 2023, https://cars.usnews.com/cars-trucks/advice/ev-charging-time.

7. Loveday, "How Long Does It Take to Charge an Electric Car?"

8. Rachel Wolfe, "I Rented an Electric Car for a Four-Day Road Trip. I Spent More Time Charging It Than I Did Sleeping," *Wall Street Journal*, June 3, 2022, https://www.wsj.com/articles/i-rented-an-electric-car-for-a-four-day-road-trip-i-spent-more-time-charging-it-than-i-did-sleeping-11654268401.

9. David Ferris, "Needed: Car Experts to Fend Off Grid Disaster," *Energywire* (blog), *E&E News by Politico*, June 12, 2023, https://www.eenews.net/articles/needed-car-experts-to-fend-off-grid-disaster/.

10. Sean McLain, "Automakers Have Big Hopes for EVs; Buyers Aren't Cooperating," *Wall Street Journal*, October 15, 2023, https://www.wsj.com/business/autos/electric-vehicle-buyer-interest-67b407cb?mod=hp_listc_pos1.

11. Tina Deines, "Toyota Is Planning a New EV with a 900-Mile Range and 10-Minute Charging Time: 'The Holy Grail of Battery Vehicles,'" *The Cool Down*, September 30, 2023, https://www.thecooldown.com/green-tech/solid-state-battery-toyota-ev-range/.

12. Brayden Wood, "Toyota's Solid-State Batteries Will Offer Over 900 Miles on a Single Charge," *Top Speed*, September 12, 2023, https://www.topspeed.com/toyotas-solid-state-batteries-up-to-932-miles/.

13. Ella Nilsen, "'Final Warning': Lawmakers, Biden Administration Sound Alarm over UN Climate Report and Urge Swift Action," CNN, August 9, 2021, https://www.cnn.com/2021/08/09/politics/un-climate-report-us-lawmakers/index.html.

14. National Oceanic and Atmospheric Administration, "Rise of Carbon

Dioxide Unabated," accessed October 29, 2023, https://research.noaa
.gov/2020/06/04/rise-of-carbon-dioxide-unabated/.

15. Air Quality Life Index, "Air Pollution: New Study Says 39 of the 50
Most Polluted Cities Globally Are in India," accessed November 12,
2023, https://aqli.epic.uchicago.edu/news/air-pollution-new-study
-says-39-of-the-50-most-polluted-cities-globally-are-in-india
/;United Nations, "India to Overtake China as World's Most Populous
Country in April 2023, United Nations Projects," accessed November
12, 2023, https://www.un.org/en/desa/india-overtake-china-world
-most-populous-country-april-2023-united-nations-projects; Meryl
Sebastian, "India's Top 1% Owned More Than 40.5% of Its
Total Wealth in 2021, According to a New Report by Oxfam,"
BBC News, January 16, 2023, https://www.bbc.com/news/world
-asia-india-64286673.

16. Lauren Frayer, "'Sunny Makes Money': India Installs a Record Volume
of Solar Power in 2022," NPR, November 21, 2022, https://www.npr
.org/sections/goatsandsoda/2022/11/21/1138409818/sunny-makes
-money-india-installs-a-record-volume-of-solar-power-in-2022; Lauren
Frayer, "India Pledges Net-Zero Emissions by 2070 – But Also Wants
to Expand Coal Mining," NPR, November 3, 2021, https://www.npr.org
/2021/11/03/1051805674/modi-india-cop26-coal-renewable-energy.

17. Julia Simon, "China is Building Six Times More New Coal Plants Than
Other Countries, Report Finds," NPR, March 2, 2023, https://www
.npr.org/2023/03/02/1160441919/china-is-building-six-times-more
-new-coal-plants-than-other-countries-report-fin;Sonja Hillgren,
"The Great Soviet Grain Robbery – 10 Years Later," *UPI*, July 30, 1982,
https://www.upi.com/Archives/1982/07/30/The-great-Soviet-grain
-robbery-10-years-later/5162396849600/; "Soviet Union," Wikipedia,
last modified November 11, 2023, https://en.wikipedia.org/wiki
/Soviet_Union; "Wheat," Wikipedia, last modified November 10, 2023,
https://en.wikipedia.org/wiki/Wheat; "Maize," Wikipedia, last modified
October 27, 2023, https://en.wikipedia.org/wiki/Maize.

18. H. Xiong, X. Wang, and X. Hu, "Research on the Duality of China's
Marine Fishery Carbon Emissions and Its Coordination with
Economic Development," *International Journal of Environmental
Research and Public Health* 20, no. 2 (2023): 1423, https://doi
.org/10.3390/ijerph20021423.

NOTES

CONVERSATION #1: KATHARINE HAYHOE

1. Drew Desilver, "The Polarization in Today's Congress Has Roots That Go Back Decades," Pew Research Center, March 10, 2022, https://www.pewresearch.org/short-reads/2022/03/10/the-polarization-in-today's-congress-has-roots-that-go-back-decades/.

2. Ellen Barry, "Climate Change Enters the Therapy Room," *New York Times*, June 22, 2023, https://www.nytimes.com/2022/02/06/health/climate-anxiety-therapy.html.

3. "When Suicidal Thinking Emerges as an Escape from the Pain of Climate Distress," *Gen Dread*, July 15, 2022, https://gendread.substack.com/p/when-suicidal-thinking-emerges-as.

4. Emma Dumain, "E&E: Climate Caucus Urges Bipartisan Action on Permitting," *PolitcoPro*, November 9, 2023, https://climatesolutionscaucus-garbarino.house.gov/.

5. https://clcouncil.org/.

6. Government of Canada, "The Federal Carbon Pollution Pricing Benchmark," accessed November 12, 2023, https://www.canada.ca/en/environment-climate-change/services/climate-change/pricing-pollution-how-it-will-work/carbon-pollution-pricing-federal-benchmark-information.html.

CHAPTER 2

1. Catherine Clifford, "BP Says Demand for Oil and Gas Will Drop Dramatically by 2050 in 'Decisive Shift,'" CNBC, January 30, 2023, https://www.cnbc.com/2023/01/30/bp-demand-for-oil-gas-to-fall-and-for-renewables-electricity-grows.html.

2. Evan Halper and Aaron Gregg, "BP Dials Back Climate Pledge amid Soaring Oil Profits," *Washington Post*, February 7, 2023, https://www.washingtonpost.com/business/2023/02/07/bp-climate-emissions-oil-profits/.

3. Michael Hiltzik, "Big Oil Companies Are Already Reneging on Their Global Warming Promises," *Los Angeles Times*, February 9, 2023, https://www.latimes.com/business/story/2023-02-09/the-big-oil-companies-are-already-reneging-on-their-global-warming-goals; Ben Elgin

and Kevin Crowley, "Exxon Retreats from Major Climate Effort to Make Biofuels from Algae," *Bloomberg*, February 10, 2023, https://www.bloomberg.com/news/articles/2023-02-10/exxon-retreats-from-major-climate-effort-to-make-biofuels-from-algae#xj4y7vzkg.

4. Hiltzik, "Big Oil Companies Are Already Reneging on Their Global Warming Promises."

5. Tucker Perkins, "Can Fossil Fuels Help Address Climate Change?" produced by Propane Education & Research Council, *Path to Zero*, February, 2022, podcast, website, 47:41, https://propane.com/environment/podcast/2-07-can-fossil-fuels-help-address-climate-change/.

6. Scott Galloway, "The Mother of All Pivots," produced by George Hahn, *Pivot*, April 28, 2023, podcast, website, 18:24, https://www.profgalloway.com/the-mother-of-all-pivots/.

7. Nader Kabbani and Nejla Ben Mimoune, "Economic Diversification in the Gulf: Time to Redouble Efforts," *Brookings*, January 31, 2021, https://www.brookings.edu/articles/economic-diversification-in-the-gulf-time-to-redouble-efforts/.

8. California Air Resources Board, "LCFS Pathway Certified Carbon Intensities," accessed October 30, 2023, https://ww2.arb.ca.gov/resources/documents/lcfs-pathway-certified-carbon-intensities.

9. Rob Nikolewski, "California's Energy Mix Is Changing but Natural Gas Is Still the No. 1 Source," *San Diego Union-Tribune*, August 25, 2023, https://www.sandiegouniontribune.com/business/story/2023-08-25/californias-energy-mix-is-changing-but-natural-gas-still-the-no-1-source.

10. Trillium Energy, "How Can Renewable Natural Gas Provide a Negative Carbon Impact?" accessed October 30, 2023, https://www.trilliumenergy.com/en/news/archive/2020/march/how-can-renewable-natural-gas-provide-a-negative-carbon-impact.

CONVERSATION #2: KEVIN LUCKE

1. Airbus, "Sustainable Aviation Fuel," accessed October 30, 2023, https://www.airbus.com/en/sustainability/respecting-the-planet/decarbonisation/sustainable-aviation-fuel.

2.   Tucker Perkins, "Renewable Fuels and the Fight Against Climate Change with Renewable Energy Group's Kevin Lucke," produced by Propane Education & Research Council, *Path to Zero*, September 2022, podcast, website, 25:48, https://propane.com/environment /podcast/3-17-renewable-fuels-and-the-fight-against-climate-change -with-renewable-energy-groups-kevin-lucke/.

3.   United States Department of Energy, "Alternative Fuels Data Center," accessed October 30, 2023, https://afdc.energy.gov/fuels/renewable _diesel.html.

4.   State of Oregon Department of Environmental Quality, "Renewable Diesel 101," accessed October 30, 2023, https://www.oregon.gov /deq/FilterDocs/cfpdieselfaq.pdf.

5.   United States Department of Energy, "Alternative Fuels Data Center."

6.   State of Oregon Department of Environmental Quality, "Renewable Diesel 101."

7.   Tucker Perkins, "Global Clean Energy's Richard Palmer on Camelina: Is It the Wonder Crop for Renewable Fuels?" produced by Propane Education & Research Council, *Path to Zero*, February 15, 2023, podcast, website, 39:25, https://propane.com/environment/podcast /4-14-global-clean-energys-richard-palmer-on-camelina-is-it-the -wonder-crop-for-renewable-fuels/.

CONVERSATION #3: RICHARD PALMER

1.   Joseph Luiz, "Alon Bakersfield Refinery Sold, to Be Used to Produce Renewable Fuel," *KGET*, May 8, 2020, https://www.kget.com/news /alon-bakersfield-refinery-sold-to-be-used-to-produce-renewable-fuel/.

CHAPTER 3

1.   Sandee LaMotte, "How to Sleep in a Heat Wave, According to Experts," *AccuWeather*, July 31, 2023, https://www.accuweather.com /en/health-wellness/how-to-sleep-in-a-heat-wave-according-to -experts/1566050?utm_source=facebook&utm_medium=news _tab&mibextid=Zxz2cZ.

Notes

2. LaMotte, "How to Sleep in a Heat Wave."

3. US Global Change Research Program, "Climate Science Special Report," accessed October 30, 2023, https://science2017.globalchange.gov/.

4. US Global Change Research Program, "Fifth National Climate Assessment," accessed November 14, 2023. https://nca2023.globalchange.gov/.

5. National Weather Service, "Hurricane Bertha," accessed November 12, 2023, https://www.weather.gov/mhx/Jul121996EventReview.

6. National Oceanic and Atmospheric Administration, "Record-Breaking Atlantic Hurricane Season Draws to an End," accessed October 30, 2023, https://www.noaa.gov/media-release/record-breaking -atlantic-hurricane-season-draws-to-end.

7. Center for Climate and Energy Solutions, "Hurricanes and Climate Change," accessed October 30, 2023, https://www.c2es.org/content /hurricanes-and-climate-change/.

8. Gary M. Stern, "Can Milford's Microgrid Keep the Power on During a Storm?" *T&D World*, March 26, 2019, https://www.tdworld.com /smart-utility/article/20972391/can-milfords-microgrid-keep-the -power-on-during-a-hurricane.

9. Jennifer Weeks, "US Electrical Grid Undergoes Massive Transition to Connect to Renewables," *Scientific American*, April 28, 2010, https://www.scientificamerican.com/article/what-is-the-smart-grid/.

10. Zeeshan Aleem, "California's Heat Wave Caused Rolling Blackouts for Millions," *Vox*, August 15, 2020, https://www.vox .com/2020/8/15/21370128/california-blackouts-rolling-power-outage.

11. The White House, "Fact Sheet: Biden-Harris Administration Announces New Standards and Major Progress for a Made-in-America National Network of Electric Vehicle Chargers."

12. Robert Walton, "Aging Grids Drive $51B in Annual Utility Distribution Spending," *Utility Dive*, July 25, 2018, https://www.utilitydive .com/news/aging-grids-drive-51b-in-annual-utility-distribution -spending/528531/.

13. Editorial Board, "S.O.S. for the US Electric Grid," *WSJ Opinion*, February 26, 2023, https://www.wsj.com/articles/s-o-s-for-the-u-s-electric-grid-pjm-interconnection-blackout-supply-renewables-subsidy-report-fossil-fuel-4cbdd56e.

14. Peter Behr and Miranda Willson, "DOE Touts Grid Expansion Plans as Operators Raise Concerns," *E&E News by Politico*, February 27, 2023, https://www.eenews.net/articles/doe-touts-grid-expansion-plans-as-operators-raise-concerns/.

15. David Gelles, "The US Will Need Thousands of Wind Farms. Will Small Towns Go Along?" *New York Times*, December 30, 2022, https://www.nytimes.com/2022/12/30/climate/wind-farm-renewable-energy-fight.html.

16. Linda Carroll, "Who Bought All the Toilet Paper? Study Suggests Who Was Most Likely to Stockpile During COVID-19," *NBC News*, June 12, 2020, https://www.nbcnews.com/health/health-news/who-bought-all-toilet-paper-study-suggests-who-was-most-n1230586.

17. Diane Cardwell, "Solar Companies Seek Ways to Build an Oasis of Electricity," *New York Times*, November 19, 2012, https://www.nytimes.com/2012/11/20/business/energy-environment/solar-power-as-solution-for-storm-darkened-homes.html.

18. Dan Walters, "CalMatters Commentary: Yes, California, We Have a Power Supply Problem," *Desert Sun*, August 30, 2020, https://www.desertsun.com/story/opinion/columnists/2020/08/30/california-rolling-blackouts-highlight-our-power-supply-problem-dan-walters-calmatters-commentary/5649511002/.

19. Naureen S. Malik, "'Ring of Fire' Eclipse This Weekend Will Send US Solar Power Plunging," *Bloomberg*, October 12, 2023, https://www.bloomberg.com/news/articles/2023-10-12/-ring-of-fire-eclipse-this-weekend-will-test-texas-solar-power?srnd=premium&leadSource=uverify%20wall&utm_source=substack&utm_medium=email#xj4y7vzkg.

20. Caleb Downs, "Shouting Matches Punctuate Growing Lines at San Antonio Gas Stations, More Than 100 Now without Fuel," *San Antonio Express-News*, September 1, 2017, https://www.mysanantonio.com/news/local/crime/article/Gas-shortages-reported-at-several-Exxon-Chevron-12163629.php#photo-14027672.

21. David Roberts, "How to Drive Fossil Fuels out of the US Economy, Quickly," *Vox*, August 6, 2020, https://www.vox.com/energy-and -environment/21349200/climate-change-fossil-fuels-rewiring -america-electrify.

22. Ben Zimmer, "I'm Going to Have to Science the Shit out of This," *Strong Language* (blog), September 16, 2015, https://stronglang.word-press.com/2015/09/16/im-going-to-have-to-science-the-shit -out-of-this/.

23. Tucker Perkins, "Colonial Pipeline Hack Exposes 3D Grid Need," Propane Education & Research Council, May 14, 2021, https://pro-pane.com/environment/stories/colonial-pipeline-hack-exposes-3d-grid -need/; Cybersecurity & Infrastructure Security Agency, "The Attack on Colonial Pipeline: What We've Learned and What We've Done Over the Past Two Years," accessed October 30, 2023, https://www .cisa.gov/news-events/news/attack-colonial-pipeline-what-weve-learned -what-weve-done-over-past-two-years.

24. Mary-Ann Russon, "US Fuel Pipeline Hackers 'Didn't Mean to Create Problems,'" *BBC*, May 10, 2021, https://www.bbc.com/news/busi-ness-57050690; David Connett, "Drone Attacks on Saudi Plant Could Hit Global Oil Supplies," *Guardian*, September 15, 2019, https://www.theguardian.com/world/2019/sep/15/drone-attack -on-saudi-hits-global-supply.

25. Dylan McCullagh, "Hacking Laptop Batteries: A New Security Threat," *CNET*, August 4, 2011, https://www.cnet.com/news/privacy /hacking-laptop-batteries-a-new-security-threat/.

26. International PtX Hub, "How Power-to-X Works," accessed October 30, 2023, https://ptx-hub.org/how-ptx-works/.

CONVERSATION #4: JEFFREY SCHLEGELMILCH

1. Tucker Perkins, "Climate Disaster Preparedness with Columbia's Jeffrey Schlegelmilch," produced by Propane Education & Re-search Council, *Path to Zero*, August 2022, podcast, website, 44:34, https://propane.com/environment/podcast/3-13-climate-disaster -preparedness-with-columbias-jeffrey-schlegelmilch/.

2. Candace Jackson, "What Is Redlining?" *New York Times*, August 17, 2021, https://www.nytimes.com/2021/08/17/realestate/what-is -redlining.html.

3. Evan Halper, "A Summer of Blackouts? Wheezing Power Grid Leaves States at Risk," *Washington Post*, June 2, 2022, https://www.washing-tonpost.com/business/2022/06/02/blackout-states-summer-heat/.

4. Katherine Blunt, "The US Power Grid Withstands the Heat, So Far," *Wall Street Journal*, July 23, 2023, https://www.wsj.com/articles /the-u-s-power-grid-withstands-the-heat-so-far-30e70a9c.

CONVERSATION #5: MICHAEL BURR

1. California Public Utilities Commission, "Resiliency and Microgrids," accessed November 12, 2023, https://www.cpuc.ca.gov /resiliencyandmicrogrids.

2. United Nations, "The Paris Agreement," accessed November 12, 2023, https://www.un.org/en/climatechange/paris-agreement.

3. Tucker Perkins, "Sustained Investment to Avoid a Climate Catastrophe with Columbia University's Bruce Usher," produced by Propane Education & Research Council, *Path to Zero*, October 9, 2023, podcast, website, 25:56, https://propane.com/environment/podcast /5-08-sustained-investment-to-avoid-a-climate-catastrophe-with -columbia-universitys-bruce-usher/.

CHAPTER 4

1. Mary Bellis, "Rudolf Diesel, Inventor of the Diesel Engine," *Thought-Co.*, April 8, 2019, https://www.thoughtco.com/rudolf-diesel -diesel-engine-1991648.

2. "Diesel Fuel," *Wikipedia*, last edited November 5, 2023, https://en.wikipedia.org/wiki/Diesel_fuel.

3. United States Environmental Protection Agency, "Criteria Air Pollut-ants," accessed October 30, 2023, https://www.epa.gov/criteria-air-pol-lutants; İbrahim Aslan Reşitoğlu, Kemal Altinişik, and Ali Keskin, "The Pollutant Emissions from Diesel-Engine Vehicles and Exhaust

Aftertreatment Systems," *Clean Technologies and Environmental Policy*, June 11, 2014, https://link.springer.com/article/10.1007/s10098-014-0793-9.

4. Adam Forrest, "The Death of Diesel: Has the One-Time Wonder Fuel Become the New Asbestos?" *Guardian*, April 13, 2017, https://www .theguardian.com/cities/2017/apr/13/death-of-diesel-wonder-fuel -new-asbestos.

5. Matt Kimberley, "Volvo Has Finally Confirmed the End of Its Diesel Engines," *CarThrottle*, May 16, 2018, https://www.carthrottle.com /news/volvo-has-finally-confirmed-end-its-diesel-engines.

6. Matthew Beedham, "BMW to Retire Iconic Diesel Engines amid Growing Regulatory Challenges," *The Next Web*, January 8, 2020, https://thenextweb.com/news/bmw-to-retire-iconic-diesel-engines- amid-growing-regulatory-challenges; California Air Resources Board, "California Takes Bold Step to Reduce Truck Pollution," accessed October 30, 2023, https://ww2.arb.ca.gov/news /california-takes-bold-step-reduce-truck-pollution.

7. "Lee Corso," Wikimedia Foundation, last updated October 21, 2023, https://en.wikipedia.org/wiki/Lee_Corso.

8. United States Department of Energy, "Flipping the Switch on Electric School Buses: Cost Factors: Module 1 (Text Version)," accessed October 30, 2023, https://afdc.energy.gov/vehicles/electric_school _buses_p8_m1.html.

9. ATA Staff, "A Heavy Dose of Reality for Electric-Truck Mandates," *American Trucking Association* (blog), April 19, 2023, https://www. trucking.org/news-insights/heavy-dose-reality-electric-truck-mandates.

10. Ivana Kottasova, "EU Was Set to Ban Internal Combustion Engine Cars. Then Germany Suddenly Changed Its Mind," *CNN Business*, March 27, 2023, https://www.cnn.com/2023/03/24/cars/eu -combustion-engine-debate-climate-intl/index.html.

CONVERSATION #6: FELIX LEACH AND KELLY SENECAL

1. "The Death of the Internal Combustion Engine," *Economist*, accessed November 12, 2023, https://www.economist.com/leaders/2017/08/12 /the-death-of-the-internal-combustion-engine.

2. Hans Greimel, "Reimagined Fifth-Gen Prius Foreshadows New Era of EV Fighters," *Automotive News*, November 20, 2022, https://www.autonews.com/technology/toyota-champions-future-hybrid-tech-new-prius.

3. Price Waterhouse Cooper, "What You Really Need to Know about Scope 3 Emissions and Your Business," accessed October 30, 2023, https://www.pwc.com/us/en/services/esg/library/scope-3-emissions.html.

CHAPTER 5

1. Scott Tinker, director, *Switch On,* Switch Energy Alliance, 2020, https://switchon.org/films/switch-on.

2. Tinker, *Switch On.*

3. Tinker, *Switch On.*

CONVERSATION #7: SCOTT TINKER

1. United Nations, "Damilola Ogunbiyi: Ending Energy Poverty Saves Lives and the Planet," accessed November 12, 2023, https://www.un.org/en/climatechange/damilola-ogunbiyi-ending-energy-poverty.

2. Tucker Perkins, "Energy Transition Complexities with Geologist Dr. Scott Tinker," produced by Propane Research & Education Council, *Path to Zero*, April, 2021, podcast, website, 56:15, https://propane.com/environment/podcast/2-12-energy-transition-complexities-with-geologist-dr-scott-tinker/.

3. Roger Pielke Jr., "The Iron Law of Climate Policy," *The Honest Broker*, June 13, 2022, https://rogerpielkejr.substack.com/p/the-iron-law-of-climate-policy.

4. Stanford University, "The Granger Revolution," accessed October 30, 2023, https://cs.stanford.edu/people/eroberts/cs201/projects/corporate-monopolies/dangers_grangers.html.

5. World Liquified Petroleum Gas Association, "Cooking for Life," accessed October 31, 2023, https://www.wlpga.org/key-focus-areas/cooking-for-life/.

Notes

6. Patrick Svitek, "Texas Puts Final Estimate of Winter Storm Death Total at 246," *Texas Tribune*, January 3, 2022, https://www.texastribune.org/2022/01/02/texas-winter-storm-final-death-toll-246/.

7. "List of Continents and Continental Subregions by Population," Wikipedia, last updated July 26, 2023, https://en.wikipedia.org/wiki/List_of_continents_and_continental_subregions_by_population.

8. A. Krishnamurthy, et al., "The Relevance of 'Nonsmoking-Associated Lung Cancer' in India: A Single-Centre Experience," *Indian Journal of Cancer* 49, no. 1 (2012): 82–88, https://doi.org/10.4103/0019-509X.98928.

9. International Energy Agency, "Net Zero by 2050," accessed November 12, 2023, https://www.iea.org/reports/net-zero-by-2050.

10. World Economic Forum, "To Reach Net-Zero Emissions, We Need to Build the World's Biggest Solar Farm Every Day until 2030," accessed November 12, 2023, https://www.weforum.org/videos/to-reach-net-zero-emissions-we-need-to-build-the-world-s-biggest-solar-farm-every-day-until-2030/.

11. Julia Simon, "China is Building Six Times More New Coal Plants Than Other Countries, Report Finds," NPR, March 2, 2023, https://www.npr.org/2023/03/02/1160441919/china-is-building-six-times-more-new-coal-plants-than-other-countries-report-fin

12. US Energy Information Administration, "Firm Power," accessed November 12, 2023, https://www.eia.gov/tools/glossary/index.php?id=F.

13. National Energy Assistance Directors' Association, "Midwinter Energy Update," January 30, 2023, https://neada.org/wp-content/uploads/2023/01/Press-Release-MidWinter-Energy-Update.pdf.

CHAPTER 6

1. National Aeronautics and Space Administration, "Voyager," accessed November 12, 2023, https://voyager.jpl.nasa.gov/.

2. Mike Falter, "45 Years of Nuclear Power: NASA's Voyager Deep Space Probe," *EE Power*, September 23, 2022, https://eepower.com/market-insights/45-years-of-nuclear-power-NASAs-voyager-deep-space-probe/.

3. Mike De Socio, "Why Solar Panels Will Likely Keep Getting Cheaper," *CNET*, September 25, 2023, https://www.cnet.com/home/energy -and-utilities/why-the-cost-of-solar-panels-will-likely-keep-falling/.

4. Paul Hawken, *Drawdown. The Most Comprehensive Plan Ever Proposed to Reverse Global Warming* (New York: Penguin, 2017), 19–21.

5. Bill Gates, *How to Avoid a Climate Disaster: The Solutions We Have and the Breakthroughs We Need* (New York: Alfred A. Knopf, 2021), 84–89.

6. Office of Nuclear Energy, "Nuclear Power Is the Most Reliable Energy Source and It's Not Even Close," accessed November 14, 2023, https://www.energy.gov/ne/articles/nuclear-power-most-reliable -energy-source-and-its-not-even-close.

7. Gates, *How to Avoid a Climate Disaster.*

8. US Energy Information Administration, "US Energy Consumption Increases between 0% and 15% by 2050," accessed November 12, 2023, https://www.eia.gov/todayinenergy/detail.php?id=56040.

9. World Nuclear Association, "World Energy Needs and Nuclear Power," accessed November 12, 2023, https://world-nuclear.org /information-library/current-and-future-generation/world -energy-needs-and-nuclear-power.aspx.

10. International Energy Agency, "World Energy Outlook 2023: Overview and Key Findings," accessed November 12, 2023, https://www.iea.org /reports/world-energy-outlook-2023/overview-and-key-findings#abstract.

11. International Energy Agency, "World Energy Outlook 2023."

12. Artem Vlasov, "Thorium's Long-Term Potential in Nuclear Energy: New IAEA Analysis," *International Atomic Energy Agency*, March 13, 2023, https://www.iaea.org/newscenter/news/thoriums-long-term -potential-in-nuclear-energy-new-iaea-analysis.

13. Yuval Boger, "The Dual-Pronged Energy-Saving Potential of Quantum Computers," *HPC & Quantum* (blog), *Data Center Dynamics*, June 26, 2023, https://www.datacenterdynamics.com/en/opinions/the -dual-pronged-energy-saving-potential-of-quantum-computers/.

NOTES

CONVERSATION #8, #9, #10, #11, #12: ROBERT BRYCE,
MEREDITH ANGWIN, SIR STEVEN COWLEY,
DR. RUSTY TOWELL, DR. STEVEN KOONIN

1. Tucker Perkins, "Is Nuclear Power the Path to Low-Carbon Energy?"
    Produced by Propane Education & Research Council, *Path to Zero*,
    May 13, 2021, podcast, website, 54:00, https://propane.com/environ-
    ment/podcast/2-11-is-nuclear-power-the-path-to-low-carbon-energy/.

2. Tucker Perkins, "Climate Change and Electric Grid Resiliency,"
    produced by Propane Education & Research Council, *Path to Zero*,
    June 22, 2021, podcast, website, 52:48, https://propane.com/environ-
    ment/podcast/2-13-climate-change-and-electric-grid-resiliency/.

3. Tucker Perkins, "Could Molten Salt Reactors Boost Nuclear Energy?"
    produced by Propane Education & Research Council, *Path to Zero*,
    August 11, 2022, podcast, website, 39:28, https://propane.com/envi-
    ronment/podcast/4-21-could-molten-salt-reactors-boost-nuclear
    -energy-a-conversation-with-dr-rusty-towell-nuclear-research
    er-and-physics-professor-at-abilene-christian-university/.

4. Tucker Perkins, "Making Nuclear Fusion a Successful Power Source
    with Princeton's Sir Steven Cowley," produced by Propane Education
    & Research Council, *Path to Zero*, June 2022, podcast, website, 41:50,
    https://propane.com/environment/podcast/4-10-making-nuclear
    -fusion-a-successful-power-source-with-princetons-sir-steven-cowley/.

5. Tucker Perkins, "A Closer Look at Climate Data with Theoretical
    Physicist Dr. Steven Koonin," produced by Propane Education &
    Research Council, *Path to Zero*, November 9, 2023, podcast, website,
    28:58, https://propane.com/environment/podcast/5-10-a-closer-
    look-at-climate-data-with-theoretical-physicist-dr-steven-koonin/.

6. US Energy Information Administration, "Firm Power," accessed No-
    vember 12, 2023, https://www.eia.gov/tools/glossary/index.php?id=F.

7. Villanova University, "Calculating Your Baseline Sigma," accessed
    November 12, 2023, https://www.villanovau.com/articles/six-sigma
    /calculating-your-baseline-sigma/.

8. Margaret Joy, "The Five 9s: Reliability & Availability," *Onsip*, accessed
    November 12, 2023, https://www.onsip.com/voip-resources/voip
    -fundamentals/the-five-9s-reliability-availability.

9. US Energy Information Administration, "US Electricity Customers Averaged Seven Hours of Power Interruptions in 2021," November 14, 2022, https://www.eia.gov/todayinenergy/detail.php?id=54639.

10. US Department of Homeland Security, "Power Outages," accessed November 12, 2023, https://www.ready.gov/power-outages.

11. US Energy Information Administration, "New York's Indian Point Nuclear Power Plant Closes after 59 Years of Operation," April 30, 2021, https://www.eia.gov/todayinenergy/detail.php?id=47776.

12. International Atomic Energy Agency, "What Are Small Modular Reactors (SMRs)?" September 13, 2023, https://www.iaea.org/newscenter /news/what-are-small-modular-reactors-smrs.

13. Office of Nuclear Energy, "Advanced Small Modular Reactors (SMRs)," accessed October 31, 2023, https://www.energy.gov/ne /advanced-small-modular-reactors-smrs; Office of Nuclear Energy, "Benefits of Small Modular Reactors (SMRs)," accessed October 31, 2023, https://www.energy.gov/ne/benefits-small-modular -reactors-smrs.

14. Oak Ridge National Laboratory, "Time Warp: Molten Salt Reactor Experiment – Alvin Weinberg's Magnum Opus," accessed November 12, 2023, https://www.ornl.gov/molten-salt-reactor/history.

15. Nuclear Engineering International, "TerraPower Begins Testing Molten Salt Technology," October 6, 2023, https://www.neimagazine .com/news/newsterrapower-begins-testing-molten-salt-technology -11199243.

16. World Nuclear News, "Dow's Seadrift Site Selected for X-Energy SMR Project," accessed October 31, 2021, https://world-nuclear-news.org /Articles/Dow-s-Seadrift-site-selected-for-X-energy-SMR-proj.

17. International Energy Agency, "Data Centres and Data Transmission Networks," accessed November 12, 2023, https://www.iea.org /energy-system/buildings/data-centres-and-data-transmission -networks; International Energy Agency, "Data Centres and Data Transmission Networks."

18. Katie Elyce Jones, "How Hot is Too Hot in Fusion?" Oak Ridge National Laboratory, accessed November 12, 2023, https://www.olcf.ornl .gov/2017/06/27/how-hot-is-too-hot-in-fusion/.

19. Annabel Cossins-Smith, "Scientists Achieve Net Energy Gain Break-through with Nuclear Fusion for a Second Time," *Power Technology*, August 8, 2023, https://www.power-technology.com/news/scientists-achieve-second-nuclear-fusion-breakthrough/.

20. Jeff Glor, "Inside an Experimental Fusion Energy Laboratory," YouTube video, 5:37, July 3, 2022, https://www.youtube.com/watch?v=dSa95AoFFz8.

21. Tucker Perkins, "Accelerating Energy Innovation to Mitigate Climate Change," produced by Propane Education & Research Council, *Path to Zero*, November 2021, podcast, website, 41:02, https://propane.com/environment/podcast/2-19-accelerating-energy-innovation-to-mitigate-climate-change/.

22. Kayley Deaton, "Pageants, Power, Progress: Miss America's Nuclear Advocacy," *Fissionary* (blog), *Nuclear Energy Institute*, September 7, 2023, https://www.nei.org/news/2023/fissionary-episode-1-miss-america-grace-stanke.

CHAPTER 7

1. Tucker Perkins, "Can Fossil Fuels Help Address Climate Change?" produced by Propane Education & Research Council, *Path to Zero*, February, 2022, podcast, website, 47:41, https://propane.com/environment/podcast/2-07-can-fossil-fuels-help-address-climate-change/.

2. Tucker Perkins, "Top 5 Energy Policy Changes to Expect in Biden's Presidency," produced by Propane Education & Research Council, *Path to Zero*, November, 2020, podcast, website, 49:22, https://propane.com/environment/podcast/episode-15-top-5-energy-policy-changes-to-expect-in-bidens-presidency/.

3. Tucker Perkins, "Climate Policy Shift with Greentech Media's Julia Pyper," produced by Propane Education & Research Council, *Path to Zero*, January 2021, podcast, website, 38:24, https://propane.com/environment/podcast/2-01-climate-policy-shift-with-greentech-medias-julia-pyper/.

4. Mathew P. Vanderburg, "Why Is the Year 536 Considered the Worst Year in Human History?" *Quora*, June 17, 2023, https://infoorb.quora.com/Why-is-the-year-536-considered-the-worst-year-in-human-history-1.

5.   David Bressan, "Study Shows How Humanity Survived the Toba Supervolcano Eruption," *Forbes*, July 12, 2021, https://www.forbes.com/sites/davidbressan/2021/07/12/study-shows-how-humanity-survived-the-toba-supervolcano-eruption/?sh=48a2a4093c81.

6.   Greg Rosalky, "Should We Invest More in Weather Forecasting? It May Save Your Life," NPR, July 11, 2023, https://www.npr.org/sections/money/2023/07/11/1186458991/should-we-invest-more-in-weather-forecasting-it-may-save-your-life?utm_source=substack&utm_medium=email.

7.   Tucker Perkins, "ABC News Meteorologist Ginger Zee Talks Conservation and Climate," produced by Propane Education & Research Council, *Path to Zero*, September 2022, podcast, website, 24:55, https://propane.com/environment/podcast/4-02-abc-news-meteorologist-ginger-zee-talks-conservation-and-climate/.

8.   Jon Sindreu, "Climate Risk Is Becoming Uninsurable. Better Forecasting Can Help," *Wall Street Journal*, October 30, 2023, https://www.wsj.com/business/entrepreneurship/climate-risk-is-becoming-uninsurable-better-forecasting-can-help-b9c94ca6?mod=hp_lead_pos10.

9.   Cara Buckley, "To Help Cool a Hot Planet, the Whitest of White Coats," *New York Times*, July 12, 2023, https://www.nytimes.com/2023/07/12/climate/white-paint-climate-cooling.html.

10. Tucker Perkins, "2023 Energy Predictions," produced by Propane Research & Education Council, *Path to Zero*, December 2022, podcast, website, 10:08, https://propane.com/environment/podcast/4-11-2023-energy-predictions/.

11. Energy Information Administration, "Energy and the Environment Explained," accessed November 12, 2023, https://www.eia.gov/energyexplained/energy-and-the-environment/where-greenhouse-gases-come-from.php.

12. Tucker Perkins, "DOE's Jigar Shah on Financing Clean Energy Projects," produced by Propane Research & Education Council, *Path to Zero*, June 2021. podcast, website, 35:02, https://propane.com/environment/podcast/2-14-does-jigar-shah-on-financing-clean-energy-projects/.

13. Catherine Clifford, "JP Morgan Executive Explains Why Decarbonization Is a 'Megatrend' That Business Can't Ignore," CNBC, August 22, 2023, https://www.cnbc.com/2023/08/22/jpmorgan-exec-why-and-how-decarbonization-became-a-megatrend.html.

14. Blackrock Investment Institute, "Managing the Net-Zero Transition," accessed November 12, 2023, https://www.blackrock.com/corporate/insights/blackrock-investment-institute/publications/net-zero-transition.

15. International Renewable Energy Agency, "Investment Needs of USD 35 Trillion by 2030 for Successful Energy Transition," accessed November 14, 2023, https://www.irena.org/News/pressreleases/2023/Mar/Investment-Needs-of-USD-35-trillion-by-2030-for-Successful-Energy-Transition.

16. Office of Energy Efficiency & Renewable Energy, "Hydrogen Fuel Basics," accessed October 31, 2023, https://www.energy.gov/eere/fuelcells/hydrogen-fuel-basics.

17. Jeff St. John, "The Problem with Making Green Hydrogen to Fuel Power Plants," *Canary Media*, October 10, 2023, https://www.canarymedia.com/articles/hydrogen/the-problem-with-making-green-hydrogen-to-fuel-power-plants?utm_source=substack&utm_medium=email.

18. Port of Seattle, "Five Fast Facts about Hydrogen," accessed October 31, 2023, https://www.portseattle.org/blog/5-fast-facts-about-hydrogen.

19. United States Energy Information Administration, "Hydrogen Explained," accessed October 31, 2023, https://www.eia.gov/energyexplained/hydrogen/production-of-hydrogen.php.

20. International Energy Agency, "Global Hydrogen Review 2022," accessed October 31, 2023, https://www.iea.org/reports/global-hydrogen-review-2022/executive-summary.

21. Will Horner, "North American Clean Hydrogen Projects Are Booming," *Wall Street Journal*, April 28, 2023, https://www.wsj.com/articles/north-american-clean-hydrogen-projects-are-booming-75a3d4ed?mod=hp_minor_pos16&utm_source=substack&utm_medium=email.

22. Nicola Jones, "From Fertilizer to Fuel: Can 'Green' Ammonia Be a Climate Fix?" *Yale Environment 360*, January 20, 2022, https://e360.yale.edu/features/from-fertilizer-to-fuel-can-green-ammonia-be-a-climate-fix.

23. Aliaksei Patonia and Rahmat Poudineh, "Ammonia as a Storage Solution for Future Decarbonized Energy Systems," *Oxford Institute for Energy Studies*, November 2020, https://www.oxfordenergy.org/wpcms/wp-content/uploads/2020/11/Ammonia-as-a-storage-solution-for-future-decarbonized-systems-EL-42.pdf.

24. "An Epic History of Oil from Ancient Times to the First World War," *Economist*, August 25, 2022, https://www.economist.com/culture/2022/08/25/an-epic-history-of-oil-from-ancient-times-to-the-first-world-war.

25. Keith Fisher, *A Pipeline Runs Through It* (London: Allen Lane, 2022).

26. University of Calgary, "Hydrocarbon Combustion," accessed October 31, 2023, https://energyeducation.ca/encyclopedia/Hydrocarbon_combustion.

27. Janusz Petowski and William Bains, "On the Potential of Silicon as a Building Block of Life," *Life* 10, no. 6 (June 2020): 84, https://www.researchgate.net/publication/342125663_On_the_Potential_of_Silicon_as_a_Building_Block_for_Life.

28. Wala A. Algozeeb, Paul E. Savas, Zhe Yuan, Zhe Wang, Carter Kittrell, Jacklyn N. Hall, Weiyin Chen, Praveen Bollini, and James M. Tour, "Plastic Waste Product Captures Carbon Dioxide in Nanometer Pores," *ACS Nano* 16, no. 5 (2022): 7284–90, DOI: 10.1021/acsnano.2c00955.

29. Josh Fischman, "2023 Nobel Prize in Chemistry Goes to Tiny Quantum Dots with Huge Effects," *Scientific American*, October 4, 2023, https://www.scientificamerican.com/article/nobel-prize-in-chemistry-2023-quantum-dots/; Graham P. Collins, "Cheaper Dots," *Scientific American*, December 5, 2005, https://www.scientificamerican.com/article/cheaper-dots/.

30. "Carbon Neutral vs Net Zero – Understanding the Difference," *National Grid*, accessed November 12, 2023, https://www.nationalgrid.com/stories/energy-explained/carbon-neutral-vs-net-zero-understanding-difference.

31. John Katzenberger, "Direct Air Capture and Storage," *Energy Innovation*, September 16, 2019, https://energyinnovation.org/2019/09/16/direct-air-capture-and-storage/.

32. "Carbon Offset Market Could Reach $1 Trillion With Right Rules," *BloombergNEF*, January 23, 2023, https://about.bnef.com/blog/carbon-offset-market-could-reach-1-trillion-with-right-rules/.

33. Sabrina Valle, "Occidental Plans up to $1 bln for Facility to Capture Carbon from Air," *Reuters*, March 23, 2022, https://www.reuters.com/business/energy/occidental-plans-275-million-2022-carbon-capture-projects-2022-03-23/.

34. Simon Evans, "Direct CO2 Capture Machines Could Use 'a Quarter of Global Energy' in 2100," *CarbonBrief*, July 22, 2019, https://www.carbonbrief.org/direct-co2-capture-machines-could-use-quarter-global-energy-in-2100/.

35. "Solar and Wind Are Growing Faster Than Fledgling Nuclear and LNG Once Did," *Bloomberg*, accessed November 12, 2023, https://www.bloomberg.com/news/articles/2023-04-03/solar-and-wind-energy-leave-the-past-growth-of-nuclear-in-the-dust?cmpid=BBD102023_GREENDAILY&utm_medium=email&utm_source=newsletter&utm_term=231020&utm_campaign=greendaily#xj4y7vzkg.

36. "Climeworks Raises $650 Million in Largest Round for Carbon Removal Startup," *Bloomberg*, accessed November 12, 2023, https://www.bloomberg.com/news/articles/2022-04-05/climeworks-raises-650-million-in-largest-round-for-carbon-removal-startup#xj4y7vzkg.

37. "A Startup Battles Big Oil for the $1 Trillion Future of Carbon Cleanup," *Bloomberg*, accessed November 12, 2023, https://www.bloomberg.com/news/features/2023-10-19/climeworks-battles-big-oil-for-1-trillion-carbon-capture-market?cmpid=BBD102023_GREENDAILY&utm_medium=email&utm_source=newsletter&utm_term=231020&utm_campaign=greendaily&leadSource=uverify%2520wall.

38. Shannon Osaka, "The Lego-like Way to Get CO2 out of the Atmosphere," *Washington Post*, November 13, 2023, https://www.washingtonpost.com/climate-solutions/2023/11/13/carbon-removal-graphyte-company/.

39. Tucker Perkins, "Climate Scientist Kevin Trenberth on Making the Biggest Difference with Climate Change," produced by Propane Research & Education Council, *Path to Zero*, April 2021, podcast, website, 54:15, https://propane.com/environment/podcast/4-18-climate-scientist-kevin-trenberth-on-making-the-biggest-difference-with-climate-change/.

40. International Churchill Society, "Their Finest Hour," accessed November 12, 2023, https://winstonchurchill.org/resources/speeches/1940-the-finest-hour/their-finest-hour/.

41. US Energy Information Administration, "More Than 60% of Energy Used for Electricity Generation Is Lost in Conversion," July 21, 2020, https://www.eia.gov/todayinenergy/detail.php?id=44436.

42. United Nations, "What is Renewable Energy?" accessed November 12, 2023, https://www.un.org/en/climatechange/what-is-renewable-energy.

43. US Energy Information Administration, "Wind Explained," accessed November 12, 2023, https://www.eia.gov/energyexplained/wind/wind-energy-and-the-environment.php.

44. Ella Nilsen, "What's Killing Whales off the Northeast Coast? It's Not Wind Farm Projects, Experts Say," *CNN*, January 20, 2023, https://www.cnn.com/2023/01/20/us/whale-deaths-offshore-wind-climate/index.html; Matthew Brown and Camille Fassett, "Criminal Cases for Killing Eagles Decline as Wind Turbine Dangers Grow," *AP News*, May 17, 2023, https://apnews.com/article/dead-eagles-wind-turbines-enforcement-biden-53ce35355433e18a27324f9254a2475a.

45. Natalia Mello, "Wind Energy Pros and Cons (The Carbon Footprint of Turbines)," *Renewable Energy Sources* (blog), 8BillionTrees, July 31, 2023, https://8billiontrees.com/carbon-offsets-credits/most-popular-types/renewable-energy-sources/wind-energy/.

46. University of Calgary Energy Education, "Betz Limit," accessed November 12, 2023, https://energyeducation.ca/encyclopedia/Betz_limit.

47. Mark P. Mills, "Inconvenient Energy Realities," *Manhattan Institute*, July 1, 2019, https://manhattan.institute/article/inconvenient -energy-realities.

48. US Energy Information Administration, "EIA Projects That Renewable Generation Will Supply 44% of US Electricity by 2050," March 18, 2022, https://www.eia.gov/todayinenergy/detail.php?id=51698.

49. Massachusetts Institute of Technology, "The Future of Solar Energy," accessed November 12, 2023, https://energy.mit.edu/research /future-solar-energy/.

50. Alexandra Witze, "How One Device Could Help Transform Our Power Grid," *ScienceNews*, August 24, 2023, https://www.sciencenews .org/article/one-device-transform-power-electical-grid-inverter.

51. Boger, "The Dual-Pronged Energy-Saving Potential of Quantum Computers."

52. Catherine Clifford, "Why a US National Electric Grid Would Be Great for the Climate – and Is Nearly Impossible," CNBC, February 22, 2023, https://www.cnbc.com/2023/02/22/why-we-need-nation wide-electric-grid-in-the-us-but-dont-have-one.html.

53. Mead Gruver, "Build Begins on Wyoming-to-California Power Line Grid amid Growing Wind Power Concern," *AP News*, June 20, 2023, https://apnews.com/article/wind-power-transmission-haaland -turbines-0bcde521d60bb6f75d9f5ffbb24c5a69.

54. Monika Sax, "Why You Haven't Seen These Wind Turbines Around (yet)," YouTube video, 8:33, July 28, 2023, https://www.youtube.com /watch?v=MrmASjNexdc.

55. "Mini Solar Panel: Ideal Power Source for Small Devices/Portable Appliances," *Economic Times*, accessed November 12, 2023, https://economictimes.indiatimes.com/small-biz/productline /power-generation/mini-solar-panel-ideal-power-source-for-small -devices/portable-appliances/articleshow/69412749.cms.

56. Rick Mills, "The Global Copper Market Is Entering an Age of Extremely Large Deficits," *Mining.com*, July 25, 2023, https://www .mining.com/the-global-copper-market-is-entering-an-age-of -extremely-large-deficits/.

57. Yusif Khan and Mari Novik, "Mining Old Sites Can Be a Shortcut to More Copper for the Energy Transition," *Wall Street Journal*, October 3, 2023, https://www.wsj.com/articles/mining-old-sites-can-be-a-shortcut-to-more-copper-for-the-energy-transition-22b3de5f?utm_source=substack&utm_medium=email.

58. "'More Conducive' Copper Will Lead to More Efficient Motors," *Drives & Controls*, October 20, 2020, https://drivesncontrols.com/news/fullstory.php/aid/6537/_91More_conductive_92_copper_will_lead_to_more_efficient_motors.html.

59. Australian Energy Market Operator, "Loss Factors and Regional Boundaries," accessed November 12, 2023, https://aemo.com.au/en/energy-systems/electricity/national-electricity-market-nem/market-operations/loss-factors-and-regional-boundaries.

60. Andrew Cote, "Why a Floating Speck of Metal Sent Scientists' Hearts Racing," *New York Times*, August 12, 2023, https://www.nytimes.com/2023/08/12/opinion/lk-99-room-temperature-superconductor.html.

61. Bill Schweber, "Are Superconducting Power Lines Still a Viable Option?" *EE Times*, July 7, 2022, https://www.eetimes.com/are-superconducting-power-lines-still-a-viable-option/.

62. Ian MacKinnon and Richard Taylor, "A Tenth of All Electricity Is Lost in the Grid. Superconducting Cables Can Help," *The Conversation*, February 6, 2023, https://theconversation.com/a-tenth-of-all-electricity-is-lost-in-the-grid-superconducting-cables-can-help-199001.

63. Aaron Steckelberg, Hannah Dormido, Ruby Mellen, Steven Rich, and Cate Brown, "The Underbelly of Electric Vehicles," *Washington Post*, April 27, 2023, https://www.washingtonpost.com/world/interactive/2023/electric-car-batteries-geography/.

64. Evan Halper, "EV Supply Chains Have a Human Rights Problem. Can Tech Fix It?" *Washington Post*, October 20, 2022, https://www.washingtonpost.com/business/2022/10/20/ev-supply-chain-battery-tracking/.

65. Evan Halper, "EV Supply Chains Have a Human Rights Problem. Can Tech Fix It?" *Washington Post*, October 20, 2022, https://www.washingtonpost.com/business/2022/10/20/ev-supply-chain-battery-tracking/.

66. "NRDC: Exhausted - How We Can Stop Lithium Mining from Depleting Water Resources, Draining Wetlands, and Harming Communities in South America," NRDC.org, April 27, 2022, accessed November 13, 2023, https://www.nrdc.org/sites/default/files/exhausted-lithium-mining-south-america-report.pdf?itid=lk_inline_enhanced-template.

67. Niraj Chokshi and Kellen Browning, "Electric Cars Are Taking Off, but When Will Battery Recycling Follow?" *New York Times*, December 21, 2022, https://www.nytimes.com/2022/12/21/business/energy-environment/battery-recycling-electric-vehicles.html.

68. Emma Woollacott, "Electric Cars: What Will Happen to All the Dead Batteries?" *BBC*, April 27, 2021, https://www.bbc.co.uk/news/business-56574779.

69. FutureTracker, "Electric Vehicle Battery Recycling," May 31, 2022, https://www.futuretracker.com/post/electric-vehicle-battery-recycling.

70. Jennifer L, "Toyota Reveals Solid-State EV Battery with 745-mile Range, Cuts Emissions by 39%," *Carbon Credits*, July 5, 2023, https://carboncredits.com/toyota-reveals-solid-state-ev-battery-with-745-mile-range-cuts-emissions-by-39/; Casey Crownhart, "What's Next for Batteries," *MIT Technology Review*, January 4, 2023, https://www.technologyreview.com/2023/01/04/1066141/whats-next-for-batteries/.

71. Guo Yingzhe, "CATL Aims to Mass Produce Sodium-Ion Batteries in 2023," *Caixin Global*, October 5, 2022, https://www.caixinglobal.com/2022-10-25/catl-aims-to-mass-produce-sodium-ion-batteries-in-2023-101955814.html.

72. Casey Crownhart, "Long-Lasting Grid Battery," *MIT Technology Review*, February 23, 2022, https://www.technologyreview.com/2022/02/23/1044962/grid-battery-iron-clean-energy/.

73. https://formenergy.com/.

74. Dawn Stover, "We're Going to Need a Lot More Grid Storage: New Iron Batteries Could Help," *MIT Technology Review*, February 23, 2022, https://www.technologyreview.com/2022/02/23/1046365/grid-storage-iron-batteries-technology/.

75. Prachi Patel, "The Age of Silicon is Here...for Batteries," *IEEE Spectrum*, May 4, 2023, https://spectrum.ieee.org/silicon-anode

-battery?utm_campaign=climatetechsubpdf;Lawrence Ulrich,
"The EV Battery Wish List," *IEEE Spectrum*, March 12, 2023,
https://spectrum.ieee.org/ev-battery-wish-list.

76. Byju's, "Physical Properties of Nonmetals," accessed November 13,
2023, https://byjus.com/question-answer/is-silicon-considered-as
-an-metal-or-non-metal/.

77. Prachi Patel, "Aviation, the Unlikely Road to Long-range EVs," *IEEE
Spectrum*, March 31, 2023, https://spectrum.ieee.org/silicon-battery
-air-taxis-evs; Amprius, "The All-New Amprius 500 Wh/kg Battery
Platform is Here," accessed November 13, 2023, https://amprius.com
/the-all-new-amprius-500-wh-kg-battery-platform-is-here/.

CONCLUSION

1. Yusuf Khan, "Net Zero Is Still Possible, but Clean Energy Spending
Must Go Faster," *Wall Street Journal*, September 26, 2023,
https://www.wsj.com/articles/net-zero-is-still-possible-but-clean
-energy-spending-must-go-faster-a14fca86.

2. United Nations, "Fast Facts – What is Plastic Pollution?" accessed
November 13, 2023, https://www.un.org/sustainabledevelopment
/blog/2023/08/explainer-what-is-plastic-pollution/; United Nations
Environment Programme, "From Pollution to Solution," accessed
November 13, 2023, https://www.unep.org/interactives/pollution
-to-solution/;Cecilia Jamasmie, "US Researchers Find Unexpected
New Source of Much-Needed Lithium," *Mining.com*, August 16,
2017, https://www.mining.com/us-researchers-find-unexpected
-new-source-of-much-needed-lithium/.

3. https://www.greenbiz.com/sarah-golden.

4. Tucker Perkins, "Do Fossil Fuel Interests Deserve a Seat at the Table?
GreenBiz's Sarah Golden's Gloves Off," produced by Propane Research
& Education Council, *Path to Zero*, April 2021, podcast, website,
1:10:33, https://propane.com/environment/podcast/2-03-do-fossil-fuel
-interests-deserve-a-seat-at-the-table-greenbizs-sarah-goldens-gloves-off/.

5. Scott Galloway, "Listen," *No Mercy/No Malice*, October 20, 2023,
https://www.profgalloway.com/listen/.

NOTES

6.   Tucker Perkins, "Challenging Prevailing Climate Change Narratives with *HuffPost*'s Alexander Kaufman," produced by Propane Research & Education Council, *Path to Zero*, September 2022, podcast, website, 37:27, https://propane.com/environment/podcast/4-05 -challenging-prevailing-climate-change-narratives-with-huffposts -alexander-kaufman/.

7.   Mac Anderson and Tom Feltenstein, *Change is Good . . . You Go First: 21 Ways to Inspire Change* (Naperville: Simple Truths, 2015).

8.   Allyson Mann, "Renewable Energy OK, but Not Too Close to Home," *University of Georgia Research*, July 19, 2021, https://research.uga.edu /news/renewable-energy-ok-but-not-too-close-to-home/.

9.   Jana Rose Schleis, "Advocates of Agrivoltaics See Solution to Land Use Conflict, Push for Farm Bill Funds," *Agri-Pulse*, August 9, 2023, https://www.agri-pulse.com/articles/19802-agrivoltaics-as-a -solution-to-land-use-conflict-research-needed.

10. Tucker Perkins, "Finding Climate Change Hope with Dr. Katharine Hayhoe," produced by Propane Education & Research Council, *Path to Zero*, March 2022, podcast, website, 40:49, https://propane.com /environment/podcast/3-03-finding-climate-change-hope-with -dr-katharine-hayhoe/.

11. Emily Foxhall, "Solar and Wind Companies Are Coming to Rural Texas. These Residents Are Trying to Keep Them Out," *Texas Tribune*, April 19, 2023, https://www.texastribune.org/2023/04/19/texas -renewable-energy-solar-wind-local-opposition/.

12. Hannah Ritchie, "The World Solved Acid Rain. We Can Also Solve Climate Change," *Scientific American*, October 25, 2023, https://www .scientificamerican.com/article/the-world-solved-acid-rain-we-can -also-solve-climate-change/.

13. World Economic Forum, "The Ozone Layer Is on the Right Path to Recovery: Here's How the World Made It Happen," September 15, 2023, https://www.weforum.org/agenda/2023/09/ozone-layer -hole-update-nasa/.

14. Joseph Henrich and Michael Muthukrishna, "The Origins and Psychology of Human Cooperation," *Annual Review of Psychology* 72, no. 1 (2021): 207–40.

15. Peter Nash, "Many Hands Make Light Work . . . Sort Of," *Medium*, January 29, 2019, https://medium.com/hoodoo-digital/many-hands-make-light-work-sort-of-6b9b87babd67.

Index

A

acid rain, 175
adaptation, 82–83, 123
affordable energy, 137–138
agrivoltaics, 174
air, better, 157–160
Airbus, 43
airline industry, 46–47
Anderson, Mac, 173–174
Angwin, Meredith, 134, 139, 144
anti-electrification, 13–14
Argentina, 165
Arhuacos, 111–112, 113–114
Aristotle, 37
Australia, 156, 165

B

Bahrain, 39
batteries, 164–166
battery electric vehicles. *See* electrified vehicles (EVs)
biodiesel fuel, 43–44, 106–107

BlackRock, 154
BloombergNEF, 158
BMW, 89
Bolivia, 165
Bond, Drew, 146
Bourdain, Anthony, 14
BP, 37, 38
Brazil, 165
British Thermal Units (BTUs), 157
Bryce, Robert, 134, 135–136, 139, 145
Buck, Pearl S., 26
building codes, 72–73
Burr, Michael, 77–86
buses, 90

C

California, 40–41, 60, 62
California Air Resources Board (CARB), 40, 41, 89
California Public Utilities Commission, 81
Camelina sativa, 48, 49, 50, 51–52, 55
carbon

intensity, 39, 40, 41, 45–46, 49–50

neutrality, 158

pricing, 34

sinks, 158

carbon dioxide (CO2), 25, 88, 159

carbon monoxide (CO), 88

Carson, Rachel, 127

charging, for electrified vehicles (EVs), 21–23

Chernobyl, 128

Chevron, 45

Chevron Renewable Energy Group, 45

Chile, 165

China, 26, 27, 118, 122–123, 137–138, 166

Churchill, Winston, 160

Cicero, 108

Clean Air Act, 88–89

climate change
action regarding, 31–33
denialism regarding, 84–85
emotions regarding, 31
magic wand regarding, 34, 83–85, 108–109, 125, 148–149
poverty and, 124

statistics regarding, 31

Climate Leadership Council, 34

Climeworks, 159

coal, 122

cobalt, 165, 166

Colonial Pipeline, 66, 86

Columbia, 111

compromise, 34–35

computational fluid dynamics (CFD), 98

conductivity, better, 163–164

conventional diesel, 41

Convergent Science, 98–99

Cooking for Life™, 116

copper, 163

COVID-19 pandemic, 30, 75

Cowley, Sir Steven, 135, 136, 137, 139–140, 142, 144

crystal ball, 149–150

Cummins engines, 107

D
Damon, Matt, 65

DarkSide, 66

decarbonization, 154

decentralization, 67–68

Democratic Republic of Congo, 165

dense energy, 135–136

Department of Energy, 60, 61

deuterium, 143

Diesel, Rudolf, 87–88

diesel fuel, 41, 63, 87–89, 90–91, 93–110

direct air capture (DAC), 158–159

direct carbon capture, 158

Doshi, Tilak, 174

Dow Chemical Company, 141

drop in fuels, 43

E

economy, energy and, 118

ecosystems, disruptions to, 73

Edison, Thomas, 154–155

Einstein, Albert, 87

electricity
    in 2050, 66–67, 162–163
    better, 160–163
    blackout effects from, 74
    challenges regarding, 101
    conversion of, 160

costs regarding, 100

decentralization of grid of, 67–68

disaster preparedness and, 133–134

diversification of, 67–68

electricity supply gap (ESG) and, 60, 64–65

extreme weather and, 59–60

grid-forming inverter for, 162

grid issues of, 60

grid reimagining of, 65–66

grid resiliency of, 73–74, 75–76

importance of, 134

microgrid for, 77–82, 85–86

resiliency awareness and, 61–64

solar power and, 62–63

source of, 53

storage challenges regarding, 101

electricity supply gap (ESG), 60, 64–65

electric transit buses, 90

electrified vehicles (EVs). *See*

also hybrid vehicles

better batteries for, 164–166

challenges regarding, 102–103

charging infrastructure for, 21

charging times of, 22–23

concerns regarding, 23–25

developments of, 104

discussion regarding, 96

hazing, 24

in heavy machinery, 105

solid-state batteries of, 24, 166

energy. *See also specific types*

adaptation of, 123

economy and, 118

magic wand regarding, 144–146

in pro-decarbonization, 17

reliability of, 122

transition challenges of, 38

transition of, by 2050, 39–41

Energy and Policy Institute, 13

Energy Commission (California), 81

energy-economy-

environment triad, 124, 125–126

Energy Information Agency (EIA), 129

energy poverty, 113–114, 116–117, 118–119, 124

energy supply gap (ESG), 78

energy transition, 117

environment, pillars of, 121

environmental, social, and governance (ESG) commitments, 61

environmentalists, 170–171

equity, of microgirds, 81–82

ethanol, 50–51

EVs (electrified vehicles). *See* electrified vehicles (EVs)

Exxon, 37, 38

F

farmers, importance of, 51

fats, oils, and greases (FOGs), 45–46

feedstocks, 50–51

Feltenstein, Tom, 173–174

Ferris, David, 24–25

fireplaces, 63–64

firm power, 122, 133–135

Fisher, Keith, 156–157

fission reactors, 139–140

Five 9s standard, 133

food, 26, 116

food security, 50–51

forecasting, 150–151

Form Energy, 167

Freling, Bob, 115

fueling stations, 21

Fukushima, 128, 139

fusion, 142–143, 146

G

Galloway, Scott, 172

gasoline, 37, 41, 63

Gates, Bill, 15, 129, 141

Germany, 91, 122

Global Clean Energy, 50, 52

global temperature, statistics regarding, 58

Golden, Sarah, 170–172

Goodall, Jane, 57

Gore, Al, 15

Granger movement, 115

graphene, 163–164

Graphyte, 159

greed, 152–155

green ammonia, 156

GreenBiz Renewable Energy Group, 170

green diesel, 46

grid electricity, 40–41. *See also* electricity

Guterres, António, 15

H

Hayhoe, Katharine, 29–35, 174

health concerns, 96–97, 118–119

heat, 52, 57–58

Henrich, Joseph, 175

heteroatoms, 157

Hiroshima, 127

Homogeneous Charge Compression Ignition (HCCI), 107–108

Hurricane Bertha, 58

Hurricane Cristobal, 58

Hurricane Fay, 58

Hurricane Harvey, 58, 63

Hurricane Isaias, 58–59

hybrid vehicles, 20–21, 24, 102–104. *See also* electrified vehicles (EVs)

hydrocarbon production, 38

hydrogen, 105, 143, 155–156

I

ice age, 150
Iceland, 159
Imai, Masaaki, 19
India, 26, 118, 122, 123
Indian Point nuclear plant,
     New York, 135–136
indirect carbon capture, 158
Indonesia, 165
Inflation Reduction Act, 21,
     60, 152
innovation, incentivizing,
     153
innovative energy, 139–140
Intergovernmental Panel
     on Climate Change
     (IPCC), 15
internal combustion engine
     (ICE), 89, 90–91,
     93–110
International Energy Agency
     (IEA), 120, 155–156
International Renewable
     Energy Agency, 154
Internet, heated
     conversations on, 31
iron, 167
iron law, 116–117, 125–126

J

Japan, 156
JP Morgan, 154

K

kaizen, 19–20
Kaizen Way, 19
Kaufman, Alexander, 172–
     173
Kolbert, Elizabeth, 15
Koonin, Steven, 137–138,
     145–146

L

LaMotte, Sandee, 57–58
Lawrence Livermore National
     Laboratory, 143
Leach, Felix, 93–110
liquid ammonia, 156
liquid fuels, 37–41, 53,
     55–56
listening, 172
lithium, 165, 166
Lovins, Amory, 128
Lubchenco, Jane, 24–25
Lucke, Kevin, 43–48

M

magic wand
 for climate change, 34,
  83–85, 108–109,
  125, 148–149
 for fusion, 146
 for nuclear energy, 144
 for renewable fuels, 54–55
 for wealth creation, 153
Manganese, 165
The Martian (film), 65
Mazda, 107–108
McKibben, Bill, 15
Mencken, H. L., 16
microgrid, 77–82, 85–86. *See
 also* electricity
miles per gallon (mpg),
 103–104
Milford, Connecticut, 59
MIT Energy Initiative,
 161–162
molten chloride fast reactor,
 141
molten salt technology,
 140–141
Mount St. Helens, 151
Muthukrishna, Michael, 175
Myers, Bob, 16

N

Nagasaki, 127
National Climate
 Assessment, 58
National Ignition Facility
 (Lawrence Livermore
 National Laboratory),
 143
National Renewable Energy
 Laboratory, 172
natural disasters, 72–73,
 74–75, 83. *See also*
 weather
Netherlands, 156
net zero emissions, 16–18,
 27, 38, 114–125
New Orleans, Louisiana, 72
New York Times (newspaper),
 31
nickel, 165, 166
nitrogen dioxide (NO_2), 88,
 89, 97
Norris Camp, Minnesota,
 80–81
nuclear energy
 in 2050, 129–130
 as affordable energy,
  137–138
 benefits of, 132–133
 costs regarding, 128

as dense energy, 135–136

discussion regarding, 131–146

as firm energy, 133–135

fusion and, 142–143

future of, 106–107

as innovative energy, 139–140

magic wand regarding, 144

overview of, 127–130

as safe energy, 138–139

widening the path regarding, 146

O

Oak Ridge National Lab, 140–141

Occidental Petroleum, 158

Ohno, Taiichi, 20

oil, 37, 39, 156–157

Oman, 39

Oxford Institute of Energy Studies, 156

P

paint, super white, 151–152

Palmer, Richard, 48–56

particulate matter (PM), 89

passwords, changing, 86

Paulson, Henry, 111

petroleum, 37

photovoltaics, 78

photovoltaic solar, 79

Pielke, Roger, Jr., 114, 116

PJM Interconnection, 60–61

plastic, 157–158

pollutants, 88–89, 96–97

potassium acetate, 157–158

Power-to-X, 67–68

pragmatists, 170–171

pro-decarbonization, 17

propane, 41, 61–64, 78–79, 80–81, 90, 106–107

Propane Education and Research Council (PERC), 13

Purdue University, 151–152

Pyper, Julia, 149

Q

quantum dots, 158

Quint, Ryan, 24–25

R

Red Lake Wildlife Management Area, Minnesota, 80–81

redlining, 75

renewable diesel, 45–46

renewable fuels, 43–48, 49–51, 54–55. *See also specific types*

renewable natural gas (RNG), 47

renewable propane, 47–48

resiliency awareness, 61–64

Rice University, 157

S

safe energy, 138–139

San Diego County, California, 79–80

San Pasqual Band, 79

Saudi Aramco, 38–39

Sawan, Wael, 37–38

Schlegelmilch, Jeffrey, 69–76, 83–85

school buses, 90

Schuller, Tisha, 38, 148

Scope 3 impacts, 110

Seadrift, 141

seawater, 143–144

Senecal, Kelly, 93–110

Shah, Jigar, 153

Shell, 37, 38

silicon, 167

Sindreu, Jon, 151

Six Sigma, 133

Skyactive X engine, 107–108

sleeping, in heat, 57–58

small modular nuclear reactors (SMNRs), 139, 140–141

sodium-ion batteries, 166–167

Solar Electric Light Fund (SELF), 115–116

solar power, 62–63, 77–78, 100, 120–121, 135, 136, 161, 162–163

solid-state battery, 24, 166

South Africa, 165

Soviet Union, 26

Stanke, Grace, 146

Stone, Andy, 148–149

storage, electricity, 101

sulfur dioxide (SO_2), 88

Sullivan, Dan, 87

superconductor lines, 164

Superstorm Sandy, 59

super white paint, 151–152

Swift, Taylor, 169

Switch Energy Alliance, 112, 121–122

synthetic aviation fuel (SAF), 43, 46

T

Tabuchi, Hiroko, 13–14

TerraPower, 141

Tesla, 17

3-D grid, 66–67, 69–76, 162

Three Mile Island, 128, 139

Thunberg, Greta, 15

Tinker, Scott, 111–112, 113–126, 166

Toba volcano, 150–151

Towell, Rusty, 135, 136, 138–139, 140, 142, 144, 145

Toyota, 20–21, 23, 24, 103, 109, 166

TransWest Express, 162

Trenberth, Kevin, 159–160

Trillium, 41

tritium, 143

2050

    batteries in, 166–167

    China in, 26, 27

    CO2 in, 25

    diesel fuel in, 90–91

    electricity in, 66–67, 162–163

    energy transition and, 39–41

    forecasting in, 151

    graphene-wrapped copper in, 164

    hydrogen in, 156

    India in, 26

    internal combustion engine (ICE) in, 90–91

    jump to, 176

    liquid fuels in, 39–41

    net zero emissions in, 27, 114–125

    nuclear energy in, 129–130

    oil in, 157

    overview of, 25–27

    propane in, 90

    solar power in, 162–163

    super white paint in, 152

    3-D grid in, 66–67

    United States in, 26

    wind energy in, 162–163

U

United Kingdom, 122, 156

United States, 26, 30, 122, 133–134

Uri (winter storm), 66–67, 117

US Energy Information Administration, 160, 161

INDEX

Usher, Bruce, 85

V

Variankaval, Rama, 154

volcano, 150–151

Voltaire, 13, 124

Voyager I and II, 127, 128

W

Washington Post (newspaper), 82, 165

weather, 58–61, 69–73. *See also* natural disasters

well-to-wheel methodology, 109–110

wind energy, 77–78, 100, 120–121, 135, 136, 160–161, 162–163

Winegarden, Wayne, 153

winter storm Uri, 66–67, 117

Wolfe, Rachel, 23–24

women, rights and freedom for, 118–119

wood-burning fuel, 63–64

Wooden, John, 147

World Liquid Propane Gas Association, 116

Z

Zee, Ginger, 151

zero-emission vehicle, regulations regarding, 101–102. *See also* electrified vehicles (EVs)